PRAISE FOR *THE NEW LEADER'S 100-DAY ACTION PLAN*

"What a book! New and experienced managers at every level will "fly" with this programmed learning."

—Bruce S. Gelb, President, Clairol; Vice Chairman,
Bristol Myers; U.S. Ambassador to Belgium (retired)

"I love this book and wish I had read it earlier in my career! Going into a new leadership role? Don't be among the 40 percent who fail in the first 18 months. Stack the odds in your favor with this practical and indispensable road map to success!"

—Sandy Rogers, former Senior Vice President,
Corporate Strategy, Enterprise Rent-A-Car and,
former Marketing Manager, Procter & Gamble and Apple Computer

"*The New Leader's 100-Day Action Plan* offers a comprehensive architecture with practical tools and techniques for new leaders to follow. I believe that leaders who utilize the advice from this book will have demonstrative business and cultural building results."

—Joe Bonito, Vice President,
Global Leadership Effectiveness, Pfizer

"One of the most basic yet comprehensive books I've read regarding the dos and don'ts of a successful onboarding process. A must read for all aspiring business leaders, from first-time CEOs to executives at every level of the organization. Also a great tool for human resources and talent management executives."

—Joe Griesedieck, Vice Chairman,
Korn/Ferry Executive Search

The New Leader's
100-Day Action Plan

The New Leader's 100-Day Action Plan

How to Take Charge, Build Your Team, and Get Immediate Results

SECOND EDITION

GEORGE B. BRADT

JAYME A. CHECK

JORGE E. PEDRAZA

WILEY

John Wiley & Sons, Inc.

Published by John Wiley & Sons, Inc., Hoboken, New Jersey
Published simultaneously in Canada.

For general information on our other products and services or for technical support, please contact our Customer Care Department within the United States at (800) 762-2974, outside the United States at (317) 572-3993 or fax (317) 572-4002.

Wiley also publishes its books in a variety of electronic formats. Some content that appears in print may not be available in electronic books. For more information about Wiley products, visit our web site at www.wiley.com.

Library of Congress Cataloging-in-Publication data:

Bradt, George B.
    The new leader's 100-day action plan : how to take charge, build your team, and get immediate results / George B. Bradt, Jayme A. Check, and Jorge E. Pedraza.—2nd ed.
        p. cm.
    Includes bibliographical references and index.
    ISBN 978-0-470-40703-5 (cloth)
        1. Leadership—Handbooks, manuals, etc.   I. Check, Jayme A.
    II. Pedraza, Jorge E.   III. Title
    HD57.7.B723   2009
    658.4'092—dc22

                                                    2008053853

Printed in the United States of America.

10 9 8 7

CONTENTS

CONTENTS

APPENDICES
CRITICAL TOOLS FOR LONG-TERM LEADERSHIP SUCCESS

ACKNOWLEDGMENTS

We did not so much write this book as discover it. To a large degree, it is the product of all the transitions that have influenced all the people who have ever influenced us. Throughout our careers, we have learned by doing, by watching, and by interacting with a whole range of bosses, coaches, peers, subordinates, partners, and clients. We end every PrimeGenesis[1] interaction with two questions: What was particularly valuable? What are your suggestions for improvement? It is amazing what you can learn by asking.

What you have in your hands was born of continuing to ask those questions. Since we wrote the first edition, we have learned that the book and the methodology are even more valuable than we had thought. Our clients and readers tell us how ideas in the book have made a difference to them at different times. We have also learned that we could make the book even more valuable by incorporating some changes. We have added chapters on positioning yourself, getting promoted from within, and further developing leadership skills after the first 100 days. We have also sharpened our tools and stories and increased the emphasis on communication. In some ways, your first 100 days are all about communication.

We would need a whole separate book to acknowledge the people who have had the most positive influence on us over the years. But we must acknowledge the contributions of our partners in PrimeGenesis up front: Bill Berman, Ed Bancroft, George Olcott, Harry Kangis, Jim Singh, Joe Durrett, Mark Hubbard, Mary Kaiser, Mary Lyn Kurish, Maureen O'Connell, Meg Bradt, Sandy Reeser, Suzanne Pennella, Thomas Yang, and especially Mary Vonnegut who helped format the tools.

[1]The authors are some of the founders of the executive onboarding and transition acceleration firm, PrimeGenesis.

We are indebted to the clients of PrimeGenesis on several levels. We are the first to admit that we have learned as much from them as they have from us. We give our clients complete confidentiality so we have masked individuals' and companies' names in the stories involving any of our clients. We are blessed to have the opportunity to work with an extremely diverse group of clients. They run the gamut from the multinational to the small, public and private, for profit and not for profit. The executives we work with come from many industries, from almost every discipline imaginable, and from many parts of the world. With every client, we have learned something new. They inspire, challenge, and teach us on a daily basis, and for that we are grateful. You can learn more about our list of clients on our web site at PrimeGenesis.com.

Finally, abounding gratitude to our editor, Richard Narramore; our agent, Jim Levine; and our friend and sometimes skipper, Philip Ruppel, who introduced us to both of them. Without those three, this book simply would not exist and you would not have the opportunity to benefit from the perspective and ideas it contains. So you should thank them, too. You will before you're done.

An Executive Summary of the Onboarding Process

Whether you are a veteran CEO taking the reins of your next organization or a new frontline supervisor, whether you are joining from the outside or getting promoted from within, *The New Leader's 100-Day Action Plan* will help you manage your leadership transition so you can take charge, build your team, and deliver better results faster than anyone thought possible. This matters because 40 percent of leaders going into new roles fail in their first 18 months.[1] (Yes, 40 percent!)

What do these failed leaders not know or see? What do they not do? Why can't they deliver? In most cases, they dig their own holes by missing one of the important tasks that must be accomplished in their first 100 days. Some don't understand the impact of their early words and actions and inadvertently send their new colleagues the wrong messages. Some focus on finding a new strategy, but fail to get buy-in and fail to build trust with their new team. Some do a lot of work and expend a lot of energy without accomplishing the one or two things that their most important stakeholders are looking for. All are unaware of some of the important steps required to achieve a successful transition. No leader wants this to happen; but it does, at an alarming rate.

---

[1] The 40 percent failure rate comes from a 1998 study by Manchester, Inc.—often attributed to The Center for Creative Leadership. Brad Smart cited a failure rate of 50 percent in his book *Topgrading* (Englewood Cliffs, NJ: Prentice Hall, 1999). Leadership IQ published a study September 20, 2005, suggesting that the failure rate is 46 percent at 18 months. In the March 2008 *Harvard Business Review*, Olson, van Bever, and Verry wrote, "35 percent to 40 percent of senior hires wash out within their first 18 months." So, 40 percent is still vaguely right.

Our fundamental, underlying concept is:

Leadership is about inspiring and enabling others to do their absolute best together, to realize a meaningful and rewarding shared purpose.

It's not about you. It's about them—those following your lead. How you set the direction and priorities and what you do to inspire and enable them is important. But what is most important is what they see, hear, feel, believe, and accomplish together as a team. Leadership is about your ability to create an environment where your team can deliver remarkable results and love doing it.

The Chinese philosopher Lao-tzu expressed this particularly well over 2,500 years ago when he said: "The great leader speaks little. He never speaks carelessly. He works without self-interest and leaves no trace. When all is finished, the people say, 'We did it ourselves.'"[2]

With that in mind, we have designed this book as an action plan, with a time line and key milestones you need to reach along the way to accelerate your success and your team's success in your first 100 days. These are distilled from insights gleaned from our own leadership experiences and from the work of our firm, PrimeGenesis, whose sole mission is to help executives moving into complex new leadership roles, as well as their teams, deliver better results faster. You will find our own and our clients' stories throughout this book (masked to preserve confidentiality). We hope you will find this to be a practical handbook that helps you know what you need to know, see what you need to see, and do what you need to do for you and your team to deliver better results faster.

Over the years, we have noticed that many new leaders show up for a new role happy and smiling, but without a plan. Neither they, nor their organizations have thought things through in advance. On their first day, they are welcomed by such confidence-building remarks as: "Oh, you're here. . . . We'd better find you an office."

Ouch!

Some enlightened organizations have a better process in place. If you are lucky, you will be associated with an organization that actually puts people in charge of preparing for a leader's transition into a

---

[2]Paraphrasing the 17th chapter of the *Tao Te Ching* by Lao-tzu.

new role. Imagine the difference when a new leader is escorted to an office that is fully set up for her, complete with computer, passwords, phones, files, information, and a 30-day schedule of orientation and assimilation meetings.

Better . . . but still not good enough. Even if the company has done this for you, if you have waited until this moment to start, you are already behind, and you have stacked the odds against yourself. Paradoxically, the best way to accelerate a transition into a new leadership role is to pause long enough to think through and put a plan in place—and then get a head start on implementing it.

We started PrimeGenesis in 2002 having noticed the difference between leaders who have a plan, hit the ground running, and make an impact on their first day, and leaders who wait until Day One to start planning. Since then, we have created and deployed a set of tools and techniques that help executives quickly and effectively transition into new leadership roles. Our work with executives has helped them and their teams deliver better results faster and reduce their failure rate from 40 percent to less than 10 percent at organizations including American Express, Cadbury, Johnson & Johnson, LexisNexis, MillerCoors, MTV Networks, Playtex, The Royal Bank of Scotland, and UBS, as well as several not-for-profit organizations.

The core principles and techniques we deploy to make our impact on senior leaders are the principles and techniques described in this book. *The New Leader's 100-Day Action Plan* is the plan we help executives develop and deliver. The tools work for leaders at any level, whether you are a veteran CEO or a new frontline supervisor.

The three main ideas are:

1. *Get a head start before the start.* Day One is a critical pivot point for people joining from outside the company. The same is true for the formal announcement of someone getting promoted from within. In both situations, you can accelerate progress by getting a head start and hitting the ground running. A little early momentum goes a long way.

2. *Take control of your message.* Everything communicates. People read things into everything you say and do, and everything you don't say and don't do. Thus you're far better off choosing and controlling what they see and hear, and when they see and hear

it, than letting others make those choices for you, or letting them happen by chance.

3. *Build a high-performing team.* The first 100 days are the best time to put in place the basic building blocks of a high-performing team. You will fail if you try to do everything yourself, without the support and buy-in of your team. As a team leader, your own success is inextricably linked to the success of the team as a whole.

Those ideas are built on a couple of frameworks of highly effective teams and organizations that we'll refer to throughout the book (see Figure I.1). It's helpful to explain them up front. First, the headlines:

- High-performing teams and organizations are built of *people, plans,* and *practices* aligned around a *shared purpose.*
- *Tactical capacity* bridges the gap between strategy and execution, ensuring that a good strategy doesn't fail because of bad execution.
- Five building blocks underpin a team's tactical capacity: *communication campaign, Burning Imperative, milestones, early wins,* ADEPT[3] people in right *roles.*

FIGURE I.I   Core Frameworks

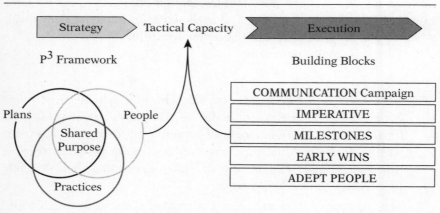

---

[3]Acquire, Develop, Encourage, Plan, Transition.

People-Plans-Practices—P³

An organization or team's performance is based on aligning its people, plans, and practices around a shared purpose. This involves getting ADEPT *people* in the right roles with the right support, getting clarity around the strategies and action steps included in *plans,* and getting *practices* in place that enable people to work together in a systematic and effective way. The heart of this is the organization's *purpose.* For that to be genuinely shared, it must be meaningful and rewarding for each of the people contributing to make its aspiration real.

Tactical Capacity

Tactical capacity is a team's ability to work under difficult, changing conditions and translate strategies into tactical actions decisively, rapidly, and effectively. It is the essential bridge between strategy and execution. In contrast to other work groups that move slowly, with lots of direction and most decision making coming from the leader, high-performing teams with strong tactical capacity empower each member to come up with and quickly implement critical solutions to the inevitable problems that arise on an ongoing basis. They build on strategy and plans with ADEPT people and practices to implement ever-evolving actions that work.

You have seen this yourself. You have been on teams with members who operate in disconnected silos, incapable of acting without specific direction from above. They may know the strategy. They may have the resources they need; but any variation or change paralyzes them. FEMA actually had run the drill on a major hurricane in New Orleans months before Katrina hit. But the plan collapsed with the first puff of wind because no one could react flexibly to a situation that was different from what they had expected.

In contrast, a great example of tactical capacity at work was the way NASA team members came together during the Apollo 13 crisis. Right from "Houston, we've had a problem," the team reacted flexibly and fluidly to a dramatic and unwelcome new reality—a crippling explosion en route, in space. They went beyond their standard operating procedures and what their equipment was "designed to do" to exploring what it "could do." Through tight, on-the-fly collaboration, the team did in minutes what normally took hours, in hours what normally took days, and in days what normally took months. This teamwork was critical to getting the crew home safely.

If you're lucky, you've been on teams where actions and results flow with great ease, where team members know what is really required and intended and support each other in making those things happen. Those teams have tactical capacity.

As the new leader, it's your job to orchestrate the alignment of people, plans and practices around a shared purpose. You must convince key people to embrace a Burning Imperative and deliver against it with a great sense of urgency. A Burning Imperative is the antidote to silos and departments that don't cooperate. Tactical capacity is not only about the team responding quickly to changes in external circumstances, it also is about team members working well with each other in support of the team's Burning Imperative.

Building Blocks of Tactical Capacity

The good news is that, as a leader in a new role, you can build tactical capacity into your team quickly by implementing five building blocks:

1. Drive action with an ongoing *communication* campaign.
2. Embed a strong *Burning Imperative*.
3. Exploit key *milestones* to drive team performance.
4. Overinvest in *early wins* to build team confidence.
5. Secure ADEPT people in the *right roles*.

The NASA team dealing with the Apollo 13 got each of these five building blocks in place, allowing it to react with tactical capacity of the highest order:

1. The culture had been strong. But everyone's *communication* reinforced the message that "failure is not an option" throughout the rescue mission.
2. The team's mission changed from "going to the moon to collect rocks" to the one *Burning Imperative* of "getting these men home alive." This was galvanizing enough (as a Burning Imperative must always be) to transcend all petty issues and focus everyone's efforts.

3. The team's *milestones* were clear: turn the ship around, preserve enough energy to allow a reentry, fix the carbon monoxide problem, survive the earth's atmosphere, and so on.

4. The carbon monoxide fix kept the astronauts alive temporarily and was the *early win* that made the team believe it could get the crew back to earth safely. It gave everyone confidence.

5. Everyone was working with the same end in mind; but they were working in different and essential *roles*. One group figured out how to turn the spaceship around. Another group fixed the oxygen problem. Another dealt with the reentry calculations and the spare crew did whatever it took.

Even though you're unlikely to jump into a situation as urgent as Apollo 13, in today's environment almost all leadership transitions are "hot landings," where you must hit the ground running to have a chance of success. Often you will need to fix something, fast. Sometimes you will have more time to plan. In most onboarding situations, you will have at least a few days to create an onboarding plan—especially if you give yourself a head start.

The 100-Day Action Plan

Here are the steps in our onboarding process. They are the chapters in this book. As Dr. Seuss advised, "be dexterous and deft, and never mistake your right foot for your left!"[4]

Part I   Create Your New Leadership Role

Chapter 1: Position Yourself for a New Leadership Role or Promotion

Positioning yourself for a leadership role is about connecting values with goals, and crossing strengths and communication. You must

---

[4]"Congratulations! Today is your day, you're off to great places, you're off and away. You have brains in your head, you have feet in your shoes, you can steer yourself in any direction you choose. You're on your own and you know what you know, and you are the guy who'll decide where to go. So be sure where you step, step with care and great tact, and remember that life's a great balancing act. Just never forget to be dexterous and deft, and never mix up your right foot with your left" (Dr. Seuss, *Oh, the Places You'll Go,* New York: Random House, 1990).

supplement your talent with learning and practice to build your knowledge and sharpen your skills over the short-, mid-, and long-term. Then, when you're ready, you need to communicate those strengths to secure the promotion or new leadership role you deserve.

Chapter 2: Sell *before* You Buy: Answer the Only Three Interview Questions

You cannot turn down a job you have not been offered. So first put your energy into getting the job offer. Remember that there are only three fundamental interview questions and be prepared to talk about your (1) *strengths*, (2) *motivation*, and (3) *fit* with the organization and the position. Remember also that interviews are not about you. They are about what you can do for those doing the interviewing. Selling is about positioning your strengths, motivation, and fit characteristics in terms of their needs.

Chapter 3: Map and Avoid the Most Common Land Mines

In general, you'll want to mitigate *organization*, *role*, and *personal* land mines before accepting a job and jump-start *relationships* and *learning* even before Day One so you can concentrate on successful *delivery* and *adjustment* after you start.

Chapter 4: Do your Due Diligence on the Organization, Role, and Fit

The ability and willingness to assess and deal with risk is often a critical differentiator between success and failure. Once you've been offered the job—and only after you've been offered the job—make sure it is right for you. This involves choosing between options and mitigating risks by answering three questions:

1. What is the organization's sustainable competitive advantage?
2. Did anyone have concerns about this role; and, if so, what was done to mitigate them?
3. What, specifically, about me, led to your offering me the job?

With those answers in hand, you can then decide if you've got a *low level of risk* that requires no extraordinary actions, *manageable risk* that you'll manage as you go, *mission-crippling risk* that you must resolve before going forward, or *insurmountable barriers* requiring you to walk away.

Chapter 5: Act Differently When You Are
Promoted *from Within*

While joining an organization from the outside involves position-ing yourself for the first time, getting promoted from within often requires repositioning yourself to people who already know you. There are three key differences when you are promoted from within versus joining from the outside:

1. *You can't control the context,* so prepare in advance and be ready to adjust as required in planned, unplanned, or interim changes, securing resources and support along the way.

2. *It is hard to make a clean break,* so take control of your own tran-sition by managing the internal announcement cascade and how key stakeholders learn about your promotion, securing your base and managing first impressions in the new role.

3. *There is no honeymoon,* so quickly accelerate team progress after the start by evolving the stated and de facto strategies, improv-ing operations, and strengthening the organization.

Part II Take Control of Your Own Start

Chapter 6: Embrace the Fuzzy Front End *and*
Make It Work for You Before You Start

The time between acceptance and start is a gift you can use to rest and relax or to get a head start on your new role. Our experience has shown that those who use this fuzzy front end to put a plan in place, complete their prestart preparation, and jump-start learning and relationships are far more likely to deliver better results faster than those who choose to rest and relax. Here are the five key steps:

1. Identify key stakeholders up, across, and down.

2. Plan your message, fuzzy front end, and first 100 days.

3. Manage personal setup so you have less to worry about after you start.

4. Conduct prestart meetings and phone calls to jump-start key relationships.

5. Gather information and learning in advance to jump-start learning.

Chapter 7: Decide How to Engage the New Culture: Assimilate, Converge and Evolve, or Shock

Be careful about how you engage with the organization's exist-ing culture, using an ACES model to determine whether you want to Assimilate, Converge and Evolve, or Shock it at the start. You need to make this choice early on because it will determine your approach to your fuzzy front end, Day One, and first 100 Days. Culture is hard to assess in advance, but you can build at least the start of a good working model by looking carefully at the "Be–Do–Say" of an organization:

- *Be:* The underpinning of culture (and integrity) is what people really are, their core assumptions, beliefs, and intentions.
- *Do:* These are things that can be seen, felt, or heard such as behavioral, attitudinal, and communication norms, signs, and symbols.
- *Say:* What people say about their culture can be found in things like mission statements and creeds. As Edgar Schein points out,[5] these get at the professed culture.

Chapter 8: Drive Action with an Ongoing Communication Campaign

Everything communicates. You can either make choices in advance about what and how you're going to communicate or react to what others do. It is important to craft your own communication plan and be clear on your platform for change, your vision, and your call to action before you start trying to inspire others. It will evolve as you learn, but you can't lead unless you have a starting point to help focus those learning plans.

- *Platform* for change: Why it's necessary to do anything differently
- *Vision* of a brighter future: How people see themselves fitting into that future
- Call to *Action:* What the audience should do next to be part of the solution

[5]See Edgar Schein, *Organizational Culture and Leadership* (San Francisco: Jossey-Bass, 1985).

Leadership is personal. Your message is the key that unlocks personal connections. The greater the congruence between your own values, intentions, actions, and words, the stronger those connections will be. This is why the best messages aren't crafted; they emerge. This is why great leaders live their messages not because they can, but because they must. "Here I stand, I can do no other."[6]

Chapter 9: Take Control of Day One: Make a Powerful First Impression

Everything is magnified on Day One, whether it's your first day in a new company or the day your promotion is announced. Everyone is looking for hints about what you think and what you're going to do. This is why it's so important to control your message by paying particular attention to all the signs, symbols, and stories you deploy, and the order in which you deploy them. Make sure people are seeing and hearing things that will lead them to believe what you want them to believe about you and about themselves in relation to the future of the organization.

Part III   Your 100-Day Action Plan

Chapter 10: Embed a Strong Burning Imperative by Day 30

The Burning Imperative is a sharply defined, intensely shared, and purposefully urgent understanding from each of the team members of what they are "supposed to do, *now*," and how this works with the larger aspirations of the team and the organization. While mission, vision, and values are often components of the Burning Imperative, the critical piece is the rallying cry that every one understands and can act on. Get this created and bought into early on—even if it's only 90 percent right. You, and the team, will adjust and improve along the way. Don't let anything distract you from getting this in place and shared—*in your first 30 days!*

Chapter 11: Exploit Key Milestones to Drive Team Performance by Day 45

The real test of a high-performing team's tactical capacity lies in the formal and informal practices that are at work across team members,

---

[6]Attributed to Martin Luther at the Diet of Worms, 1521, when asked to recant his earlier writings.

particularly around clarifying decision rights and information flows.[7] The real job of a high-performing team's leader is to inspire and enable others to do their absolute best, together. These leaders spend more time integrating across than managing down. The milestone tool is straightforward and focuses on mapping and tracking and what is getting done by when by whom. High-performing team leaders take that basic tool to a whole new level, exploiting it to inspire and enable people to work together *as a team!*

Chapter 12: Overinvest in Early Wins to Build Team Confidence by Day 60

Early wins are all about credibility and confidence. People have more faith in people who have delivered. You want your boss to have confidence in you. You want team members to have confidence in you, in themselves, and in the plan for change that has emerged. Early wins fuel that confidence. To that end, identify potential early wins by day 60 and overinvest to deliver them by the end of your first six months—*as a team!*

Chapter 13: Secure ADEPT People in the Right Roles with the Right Support by Day 70

Make your organization ever more ADEPT by Acquiring, Developing, Encouraging, Planning, and Transitioning talent:

- *Acquire:* Recruit, attract, and onboard the right people
- *Develop:* Assess and build skills and knowledge
- *Encourage:* Direct, support, recognize, and reward
- *Plan:* Monitor, assess, and plan career moves over time
- *Transition:* Migrate to different roles as appropriate

This is one of the most important things you do. Jump-start this by getting the right people in the right roles with the right support to *build the team!*

---

[7]Neilson, Martin, and Powers, "The Secrets to Successful Strategy Execution," *Harvard Business Review,* June 2008, page 60.

Chapter 14: Evolve *People, Plans, and Practices to Capitalize on Changing Circumstances*

By the end of your first 100 Days, you should have made significant steps toward aligning your people, plans, and practices around a shared purpose. Remember, this is not a one-time event but, instead, something that will require constant, ongoing management and improvement.

- Manage your organization (people) by deploying the ADEPT tool for ongoing talent development. You don't have to use this tool. But you do have to have a complete and disciplined way to strengthen your organization on a continuous basis over time.

- Manage your strategy (plans) as a cycle, ensuring you are looking at your situation, customers, collaborators, capabilities, competitors, and conditions on a regular basis and reflecting changes in them in your ever-evolving strategies and plans.

- Manage your operations (practices) by continually tracking, updating, and adding milestones. Disciplined, integrated execution doesn't happen unless you demand it, monitor it, and reinforce it over and over again.

Monitor the situation over time. Identify and classify the impact of surprises as major or minor, enduring or temporary, and be ready to react as appropriate. For major, temporary events, follow the basic flow of prepare—understand—plan—implement—revise or prepare. For major, enduring changes, redeploy or restart with relentless control of the message throughout.

Make This Book Work for You

By now you should be aware that there may be a better way to manage transitions than just showing up on Day One or charging into your promotion announcement or newly merged team and doing what "they" tell you to do. Similarly, there may be a better way for you to tackle this book than just starting on page one and reading straight through until you lose steam.

You might want to start with the 100-Day Checklist (Tool 6.1) at the end of Chapter 6. You might want to begin with the chapter summaries at the end of each chapter. Or you may prefer to read straight through the main body of the book. Use the book's elements in the way that works best for you. Just bear in mind that there really is a logical order of thinking and acting here, and it is helpful to have this clear in your mind before you do anything. Don't read this book over your first 100 Days. Read the most appropriate parts now, and then dip back in repeatedly over your 100 Days and beyond.

We have designed this as a flexible handbook split into a main body and set of appendixes. The main body (Chapters 1 through 14) is highly structured and practically oriented, with ideas, examples, tools, forms, and checklists in the book, and with easily downloadable, modifiable, and printable versions of them online. In this main body, we are highly prescriptive and directive: "Do this," "Do that," "Don't do the other."

Our first prescription is that you should *not* follow our prescriptions—or at least not all our prescriptions in all situations. Instead, take the pieces that generally work for you and adapt them as appropriate for your specific situation. People have found that these ideas work for leaders going into new companies, getting promoted from within, merging teams, as well as in situations where it's appropriate to hit a restart button. Since everything is always changing, we could all lead better with an ongoing series of 100-Day action plans.

The appendixes provide more depth on a couple of important subjects, more exploration of the theoretical underpinnings of the 100-Day Action Plan, and some additional ideas that you may find useful over time. Where the main body of the book takes full aim at actions for your first 100 Days, the appendixes put those actions in the context of things that will take longer to play out. It is not that the information in the appendixes is less important. It is just less urgent.

People often tell us, "This is just common sense. But I like the way you've structured it." As you set out to follow our structure, understand that we have a bias to push you to do things faster than others would expect. This timetable is based on the needs of our clients, who typically are moving into demanding, complex new leadership roles, and who need to meet or beat high expectations fast; but it may not be appropriate for your situation without some customization. We present you with options and choices. You are in charge. We wish you success in your new leadership role. We hope this book will help you and your team deliver better results faster than anyone thought possible!

CREATE YOUR NEW LEADERSHIP ROLE

CHAPTER I

Position Yourself for a New Leadership Role or Promotion

Part I—POSITION and SELL yourself; MAP and AVOID land mines, Do your DUE DILIGENCE

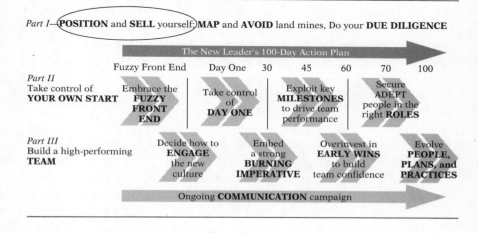

T here are two dimensions to activating your leadership potential. The first is understanding and declaring your own leadership qualities and capacities. The second is interacting effectively with others in such a way that it becomes part of an organization's or a market's perception of you. Know yourself, and then help others know you. We have mapped out concrete steps you can take to *position* yourself for leadership roles and promotions.

Begin with the first dimension—know and declare yourself a leader. The "declaring" part is important since this is what best enables you to commit to your career path. Start by declaring this to yourself. Commit yourself. Your commitments become more real, however, when you share them with others. Select a listener or buddy or two and declare your intentions and your commitments to them. They are suddenly that much more real.

3

Next, build a career plan. Great leaders are not made in a day. Leadership is built. We have developed a tool called the *Five-Step Career Plan* that can help you know yourself professionally, stake out your career path, and set yourself in motion.

The Five-Step Career Plan

This tool provides a quick and effective way to help you understand what makes you tick professionally and design a career trajectory for yourself. Use it to learn your strengths, values, and interests, and to help you align your professional choices and behavior with those qualities.

There is a downloadable, printer-friendly copy of this tool (and of many of the tools in this book) at www.onboarding-tools.com. You may find it more effective to write notes on your copies than to write in the book.

Let's walk through the main steps.

1. *Likes and dislikes:* This is your raw data. Go through your past activities and jobs and lay out everything you liked and didn't like. This is about specifics, not generalities. It may help to use the third person, as in the following examples, when making your list. *She* liked: planning, thinking, getting a sense of accomplishment, working with people she liked, having some freedom, relying on the support system of a big company, having a short commute, not working on weekends. *He* didn't like: being pushed too hard, not being able to take Sunday off, dealing with things that didn't work right, having colleagues let him down, feeling as if he worked at a company of second-class citizens. People tend to enjoy doing things they are naturally strong in. This exercise will help you understand your strengths. Dig underneath to pull out the values that underlie some of your likes and dislikes.

2. *Ideal job criteria:* With these values in mind, lay out your ideal job criteria. If you could wave your magic wand, what would that your dream job look like? Explore what features of these criteria are meaningful or important to you. Test, challenge, and shape your answers. Make sure the criteria line up with your strengths, values, and interests.

3. *Long-term goals:* Next, consider your long-term goals. It may help to start at the end, say retirement, work back 10 years, then 5 years, then 3 years. What do you want to achieve? Think about

your professional life and about your personal life, and especially about the ways these are connected. Throughout all this, you should be connecting your strengths, motivations, and criteria for fitting your goals. You may feel you have a good sense of these before you start. Or you may feel that these are too removed from the practical job at hand. Either way, go through this exercise, and open yourself to these questions: What matters to you now? What will matter to you over time?

4. *Options:* The idea of options triggers widely different responses in people. Some people become oddly passive, or even fatalistic. "What will be will be." And then, "Well, it was meant to be." Others panic, get jumpy. We urge a different approach. We are convinced that the mindset that generates a sense of possibilities and options is the mindset that *creates* opportunities and fosters success. We encourage you to read Appendix I—Leadership. This should enrich your sense of how to create leadership options for yourself.

   And not just one option! Options energize potential. Create parallel options for yourself. Real ones. Even if your second option is not nearly as attractive as the main option at hand, having a viable alternative is crucial to your success in negotiating the first option and can help you see the apparently preferred option in a better light.

5. *Choice:* If you follow these suggestions, sooner rather than later an opportunity will come your way. If you've done your homework, you will have at least two real options to choose from when the moment comes to make a decision. Go back to your list of ideal job criteria and long-term goals. Look at your options. Think through what they are really likely to bring you. Compare options by weighting your criteria and evaluating each option's results.

6. *Gut check:* Once you've made your choice, write it down and go to sleep. If you wake up in the morning feeling good, then you've probably made a good decision. If you wake up in the morning with your gut indicating that you have made a mistake, you misled yourself. Most likely, you erred in weighting your ideal job criteria. It's okay to mislead yourself, as long as you have the maturity and mechanism to make you aware of it. Your gut is that mechanism.

The basic steps are (1) understand yourself and your goals, (2) create options, (3) select the best option. You can run this over a short-term, mid-term, or long-term time frame.

Over the *short-term*, you can't change your strengths. You are what you are and should focus on creating options that can take advantage of your existing strengths. This means you should concentrate on understanding your own strengths and then helping others understand them. If communicating is not one of your strengths, start working on that skill right away. Leadership and communication are inextricably related. Buying a lottery ticket might give you a better chance at winning leadership opportunities than trying to succeed with poor communication skills.

Over the *mid-term*, you can sharpen your existing skills and knowledge and take a slower approach to bringing them to others' attention. Get yourself involved in projects both inside the company and outside the company that stretch you so you can learn and practice. If you are proactively building your strengths, people often take it as a sign that you are meant for leadership. Finally, help others who might advance into positions down the road where they can help you.

Over the *long-term*, decide what strengths you'll need to achieve your long-term goals. As Charon and Drotter discuss in *The Leadership Pipeline*,[1] different strengths are required to manage yourself, manage others, manage managers, manage functions, or manage an entire business. Virtually all the leaders we've ever talked to readily admit that, along the way, they learned a lot that they needed to know, even—believe it or not—newly minted MBAs with pedigrees that suggest they are ready-made leaders. Thus, if you want to move to different levels of leadership over time, you will need to supplement your existing talents with new strengths, knowledge, and skills. With a long-term view, you can and should invest in appropriate learning and in getting yourself into positions and assignments that allow you to practice new leadership skills.

Communicating Leadership

Now, the second part: "Help others know you." Once you've gotten a good handle on your strengths and your goals, you are ready to think through positioning in a proactive and methodical way. The simple exercise of knowing your strengths and goals will set in motion a leadership dynamic whereby you signal your leadership qualities to others, they attribute these qualities to you, and opportunities for

---

[1]See Charan, Drotter, Noel, *The Leadership Pipeline* (San Francisco: Jossey-Bass, 2001).

leadership emerge. The point here is to make this make this a deliberate and conscious plan.

We have broken down the components of communicating leadership into a set of six basic elements that you should deploy deliberately and consistently. Here are the headlines. See Appendix I for more discussion.

1. Listen first.
2. Talk in order to listen and connect better.
3. Imagine the leaders' or key stakeholders' perspective.
4. Identify potential areas for leadership.
5. Lead through:
   a. Work,
   b. Insight,
   c. Reliability,
   d. Judgment,
   e. Energy,
   f. Humor,
   g. Conflict,
   h. Crisis,
   i. Inspiration.
6. Carpe diem.

Position Yourself—Summary and Implications

Start by understanding your existing strengths and talents that you can be turn into strengths appropriate to meet your long-term goals (see Tool 1.1).

- *Short-term:* You can't change your strengths. Do things to let others know about your strengths.
- *Mid-term:* You can sharpen existing skills and knowledge. Do projects that stretch you.
- *Long-term:* You can build new skills and knowledge. Look for assignments that allow you to learn and practice new things.

Then communicate your readiness for leadership by leading something, whether it's a major project or the team outing.

Downloadable TOOL 1.1
Five-Step Career Plan*

1. List your *likes and dislikes:*

Activities

_____

_____

Jobs

_____

_____

Situations

_____

_____

Lifestyle

_____

_____

Other

_____

_____

2. List your *ideal job criteria* categorized as follows:

Good for others (impact on others, match with personal values, influence on organization)

_____

_____

Good for me (enjoyable work/activities, fit with life interests, reward, recognition, respect)

_____

_____

Good at it (match between activities and strengths, learning, development, resume builder)

_____

_____

   Life interests:
   Application of technology
   Quantitative analysis
   Theory development, conceptual thinking
   Creative production
   Counseling and mentoring
   Managing people and relationships
   Enterprise control
   Influence through language and ideas

3. Identify your *long-term goals*:

_____

_____

4. Build a broad range of *options* that meet your long-term goals:

_____

_____

5. Make *choices* by evaluating your options against your criteria:

_____

_____

Finally, perform a *gut check.*

CHAPTER 2

Sell Before You Buy

ANSWER THE ONLY THREE INTERVIEW QUESTIONS

Part I—POSITION and SELL yourself; MAP and AVOID land mines, Do your DUE DILIGENCE

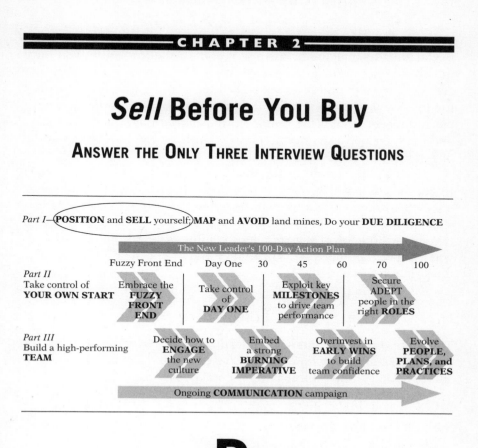

R emember three things during the interview process:

> *Thing 1:* You cannot turn down a job offer that you have not received.
>
> *Thing 2:* There are only three fundamental interview questions—ever.
>
> *Thing 3:* There are only three fundamental interview answers—ever.

Thing 1

Before you accept a job, you must first get an offer. Then, and only then, you can decide if you should accept it. Do not do these steps out of order. Your initial focus should be solely on getting the job offer. If you start to imagine or assume you have the job before you have the offer, you have diverted some of your focus away from reality and are wasting your time. Get your head back in the game. First comes the interview, and then comes the offer. It is important that you realize and respect that clear demarcation between the interview process and the offer because once you cross that line (you have received the offer), your approach should change.

Everything you do in the interview process should be designed to get the company to offer you the job. This includes not only your answers to their questions, but also your questions to them. At this stage in the process, your questions are not about helping *you* decide if you want the job. They are about helping *them* decide to offer it to you. Secure the offer first. Then, after you've got the offer, figure out if it's right for you.

Thing 2

There are only three interview questions. Every question you've ever been asked, and every question you've ever asked in an interview is a subset of one of these three fundamental questions:

1. Can you do the job?
2. Will you love the job?
3. Can I tolerate working with you?

That's it. Those three. The questions may be asked in different words, but every question, however worded, is just a variation on one of these. As each question comes, it is your job to determine which of the three is really being asked.

Thing 3

Since there are only three fundamental interview questions, there are only three fundamental interview answers. Every answer you give in an interview should be a subset of these three answers:

1. My *strengths* are a match for this job.
2. My *motivations* are a match for this job.
3. I am a good *fit* with this organization.

That's it. Those three. Your answers to questions will be more elaborate, but your answers should always be dressed-up versions of one of the three.

Since there are only three interview questions and three interview answers, all you have to do is to prepare three answers in advance and recognize what question you are being asked. Then you are ready to ace any interview. If Question 1 is asked, you should lead your response with an Answer 1. Question 2 indicates that you lead with an Answer 2. You're probably catching on by now, but a Question 3 requires you to lead with an Answer 3. Simple huh? After you lead with the proper answer you can embellish your response with either of the other two answers.

The bad news is that it is going to be a lot more work than you might think to prepare these answers in advance of each interview. Interviews are exercises in *solution selling*. They are not about you. If you've figured out your own strengths, motivations, and fit criteria, and if you've gotten in front of the right people at the right organizations, then you're selling. Think of the interview process as a chance for you to show your ability to solve the organization and interviewer's problem. That's why motivation is about how your values and what you like to do *fit with the role*. That's why you need to highlight strengths in the areas *most important to the interviewers*, and why you must *position their organization* in terms of fit with your values. Thoughtful preparation can often be the deciding feature between a yes and a no. This is tricky stuff. It is worth the investment of time.

Question 1: Can you do the job? Or more likely: What are your strengths? (Strengths)

Answer 1: Prepare three situation/action/results examples that highlight your strengths in the *areas most important to the people interviewing you*.

Question 2: Will you love the job? Or more likely: What are you looking to do? (Motivation)

Answer 2: Position the *role* you are applying for in terms of your values and what you like to do.

Question 3: Can I tolerate working with you? Or more likely: What sort of people do you like to work with? (Fit)

Answer 3: Position the *organization* you're interviewing with in terms of your values and the people with whom you like to work.

Imagine you are interviewing for a job where a new leader and a new team are being put together to solve a specific problem or address a specific need or goal. The parties doing the interviewing may not fully understand the problem; and if they do, they may not fully articulate it to you during the interview. In many cases, organizations think and learn about what they want as they conduct the hiring process. You can have a greater impact than you realize on what the organization needs and what the job should be at this point. The winning candidate is often the one who, acting as a management consultant, helps the decision makers and team members get a better sense of what the problems, or needs, really are, and then conveys confidence that under the candidate's supervision the right things would get done.

Let's return to the three interview questions and answers. Since you have done your homework, all you have to do is figure out which of the three questions you are really being asked, and respond to it with the corresponding answer. You should always lead with the corresponding answer to the question, but from there you can move on to other answers. Skillful candidates can transition smoothly from the topic at hand, whatever it is, to the key points they want to cover. The key points should always indicate that the candidate is a solid fit for the role. You want to talk in terms of strength, motivation, and fit, but you may not want to use those words or reveal your approach. In fact, we recommend that you don't. Think of this approach as a secret code.

The powerful part of this approach is that the interviewer will never know you are deploying it and your answers will tell an impressive story, regardless of the interviewer's skill level. By knowing this secret code of interviewing, you can control the process without anyone realizing you are doing so. Don't be afraid to lead the interview by deciphering the real questions beneath the actual questions and then providing the corresponding answers.

For example, "Tell me about yourself." Make no mistake about it, this is a strengths question and you should lead with a strengths-based answer. This common but somewhat dauntingly open-ended question can also be leveraged as a setup for all three of your answers. The joking-chatting time is over; you've been given the reins for a bit. Be ready to lead the interview process with your strengths and let the interviewer guide you to motivation and fit.

"What do you know about me/us?" This is a motivation question if there ever was one. Prove that you cared enough to do some homework. You should know, or have surmised, enough about their current situation to put you in a position to discuss your strengths and fit as well.

Chart 2.1 lists some common interview questions and classifies them into their proper categories.

CHART 2.1   The Questions Behind the Questions

Common Question	Real Question	Lead Answer
Tell me about your career transitions.	Will you love the job?	Motivation
Tell me what you did at _____?	Can you do the job?	Strengths
Tell me about your favorite boss.	Can I tolerate working with you?	Fit
Why should we hire you?	Can you do the job?	Strengths
What is your greatest weakness?	Can you do the job?	Strengths
Are you a team player?	Can I tolerate working with you?	Fit
Why did you leave your last job?	Can I tolerate working with you?	Fit
Where do you see yourself in five years?	Will you love the job?	Motivation
Why does this job interest you?	Will you love the job?	Motivation
What would your last team say about you?	Can I tolerate working with you?	Fit

The "strengths, motivation, fit" concept is a good organizing tool for your interview preparation. But remember that you probably don't want to show your organizing tool to interviewers unless it reinforces one of the strengths they are evaluating.

Champion athletes know that the race begins long before the starting gun is fired. While this is a cliché in the world of sports, it's barely recognized in the business world. It is startling how rarely executive leaders make the most of the early stages of onboarding and particularly those first contacts with the new organization.

So here's our tip: Your new assignment started as soon as you learned you were a candidate. Act accordingly. Be prepared. Strategize. Spend the time and effort that you would if you had already started the job. You wouldn't walk into a presentation to the board of directors unprepared, would you? Each interaction with the people involved in hiring, evaluating, and working with you should bear the marks of careful and thoughtful preparation, delivery, and follow-through. You are making many critical first impressions. Patterns of perception and behavior are being set as soon as you become a candidate. You should be the one to script them. Carefully plan and prepare for each of your meetings during the hiring process.

If you've been involved in hiring a new leader, then you know that those involved in the decision can have wildly different ideas about what to look for in the candidate. If you're lucky, you have experienced seeing a great candidate emerge from an interview process. You're even luckier if this person ended up being what people had hoped.

How does a great candidate emerge and why? What usually happens is that the candidate somehow manages to hit the right buttons for two or more people in the process, and those interviewers begin to influence the process on the candidate's behalf. How did that happen? Chance? Possibly, but skill is also likely to have been involved. The candidate presented strengths and motivation in a way that directed the discussion onto the question of fit. How do skillful candidates do this? A standard technique is to structure the interview as an exchange where as much information is being given as is being put out. As in any selling situation, there needs to be a back-and-forth flow of queries, expressions of interest, thoughtful answers, and enthusiasm.

Great job candidates foster enthusiasm in the people who are interviewing, and that enthusiasm in turn gives those candidates a lot of insight and allows them to sell themselves more effectively. How do you foster enthusiasm? By presenting yourself with confidence and professionalism, certainly, but also by being enthusiastic. Great candidates enjoy the interview process. They come across as if they really enjoy talking about work, management styles, the opportunities at hand, and other related topics. This is not to be confused with an attempt to behave like a cheerleader waving pom-poms. A skillful interviewer helps set up the conditions for discussing things that matter. What's important to you and what's important for them, coupled with what really motivates you and what really motivates them are what matter. For your interview to be successful, you must find a way to compellingly and enthusiastically communicate those things that matter.

Come prepared, present with confidence, be enthusiastic (talk about what matters), and brim with a sense of possibility and opportunity. These qualities will quickly attract an inside ally, which is often the way opportunities get offered to you.

HOT TIP

Everything **is part of the interview:** You won't go too far wrong if you imagine that everything you do and say is being videotaped to be shown to the final decision maker. This is why you must use every part of every interaction with everybody in the organization as an opportunity to reinforce your strengths, motivation, and fit. Until you've been offered a job, it's all about getting the offer.

Be "On" at All Times When Being Considered for a Promotion from Within

Management will be looking at your strengths, motivation, and fit when they are considering you for promotions from within as well. So you'll want to use the same strategy as previously discussed when you are being interviewed. *But*, and it's a big but, they may not ever interview you. Instead, they may get answers to questions in these areas by observing you in your job or through a series of casual conversations with you or with others. So, if everything is part of the interview when you're joining from the outside, it's equally true that everything is part of the overall evaluation when you're up for a promotion from within. Often this evaluation will be going on before you even know that you're up for a promotion. So, our prescription is to assume that you're always being evaluated for the next promotion. More strategies for getting promoted from within are discussed in Chapter 5.

Negotiate for Success

You got the offer! Congratulations! You're done! Accept it and move forward. Right?

Wrong! Don't relax yet. There's often a real sense of urgency on the part of the hiring organization to move as quickly as possible from offer, to acceptance, to start. It is a huge trap that can be detrimental to you should you get caught up in it. Even with the initial offer in hand, there are things you need to do to set yourself up for success. The goal is to set things up for a successful outcome over the long-term. As any mogul skier knows, if you're focusing only on the bump you're just going over, the next one can throw you off. Look ahead.

You may have to shape that offer to turn it into a recipe for success. First you *sell* to get an offer. Then you *negotiate* to get the right offer. Then you do a thorough *due diligence* to decide whether you should accept. It is important to do these in sequence so that you don't muddle your thinking or send mixed messages. With the offer in hand, selling is over. Let's deal with negotiating here. We'll tackle due diligence after we lay out the risks of onboarding. (In the real world, negotiating and due diligence often overlap. That's okay. Just don't start either until you're done selling.)

You must negotiate a win-win package factoring in all the different forms of short-, mid-, and long-term compensation, benefits, termination rights, and the like. It is equally important to negotiate the details of the role as well as responsibilities, expectations, and authority. There are generally more dimensions open to negotiation than are readily apparent. Take a hard look at the position's responsibilities and relationships. Make sure they line up with appropriate authority and resources. If there's a mismatch, negotiate to correct it here and now or pay the price later. While it's great to get any offer, the first offer may be just one step toward crafting the *right* offer.

Many people find negotiating for job terms unpleasant, possibly even distasteful; it makes them nervous. In the face of this nervousness, people may resort to uncharacteristic behavior. They become oddly passive. Or oddly aggressive, playing out some imagined role from the *Godfather*. We could write a separate book about negotiating; but for now, suffice it to say that it can and should be done in a positive, constructive, collaborative atmosphere and tone. It is about clarifying needs and desires for both parties. Successful negotiations typically leave both parties energized, and there is no situation where this is more important than in negotiating for a new job responsibility.

Having completed the negotiations, it's time to make your final choice. Go back to the Five-Step Career Plan (see Chapter 1) and go through the choice and gut check steps.

Negotiating Worksheet

Once you've been offered your new position, the negotiating begins. To ensure that you address all the issues that are essential to your success, follow our six-step process on negotiating:

1. *Make a plan*. (Identify the dimensions of the negotiations by answering these questions: What are my needs and concerns? What are the employer's needs and concerns?)
2. *Get started*. (Identify areas of agreement.)
3. *Clarify positions*. (State, support, and listen.)
4. *Find alternatives*.
5. *Gain agreement*. (Study proposals, make concessions, summarize, and test the agreements.)
6. *Implement*. (Communicate, deliver, and monitor.)

Make a Plan

There are two parts to this, mapping out your needs and concerns, and mapping out their needs and concerns across the critical dimensions of the negotiation. Your dimensions reflect your ideal job criteria and long-term goals. It's important to know what you want and what you're willing to give up to get it. To complete this process, identify your walkaway, minimum, expected, and opening points for each critical dimension for you and for the employer.

For You

- "Walkaway" is the minimum you'll even begin to talk about. If the other party opens with something below that point, you walk away without even countering.
- "Minimum" is the minimum acceptable.
- "Expected" is where you think a deal will be done.
- "Opening" is what you'd say first, if asked.

For Them

- "Walkaway" is the maximum they'll even begin to talk about. If you open with something above that point, they walk away without even countering.
- "Maximum" is the maximum acceptable.
- "Expected" is where they think a deal will be done.
- "Opening" is what they'd say first, if asked.

In this example, on the dimension of base salary, there is a deal to be done. You, the new leader are expecting a base salary of $225,000, but would take as low as $205,000. The company is expecting to pay you $210,000, but would pay as much as $230,000. Thus, there is a deal to be done somewhere between $205,000 and $230,000.

The dimensions are important. The more dimensions you can negotiate on, the more room there is for give-and-take. For many people, a $200,000 straight salary is not as good as a $190,000 salary with a $10,000 per year travel allowance, or a salary of $190,000 and a bonus of up to $25,000. As the level of the role increases, the degrees of freedom on negotiations increase as well. A good way to learn what's possible is to pull recent employment contracts off the Web for senior leaders of the company.

One executive got bored with his retirement. He applied for and was offered a job in a consulting group with compensation of a straight salary. His response was "That's much less than I've been used to earning. But, given my stage in life, I could be happy with that annual salary if you gave me 20 weeks' vacation a year." They did.

We've used a base salary example because it's easy to illustrate. You will want to map out on similar scales all the important dimensions of short-, mid- and long-term compensation, benefits, termination rights, role, responsibilities, expectations, and authority (see Figure 2.1).

Sell before You Buy—Summary and Implications

- Get the offer first. You cannot turn down an offer you have not received.

- Prepare for an interview by being ready to position your strengths, motivation, and fit in the context of the interviewing organization's articulated and unarticulated needs.

- In the interview, make your points fully, but succinctly, and then shut up and listen.

- In your normal, day-to-day work, act and talk as you would if you were being evaluated for a promotion. (Because you are.)

FIGURE 2.1   Negotiating Map

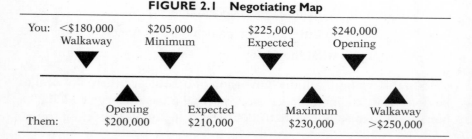

You:	<$180,000 Walkaway	$205,000 Minimum	$225,000 Expected	$240,000 Opening
Them:	Opening $200,000	Expected $210,000	Maximum $230,000	Walkaway >$250,000

QUESTIONS YOU SHOULD ASK YOURSELF

- Have I thought through multiple examples of how I can answer the three key questions?
- Have I taken a thoughtful approach to acceptance and negotiation?
- Is this job right for me in terms of strength, motivation, and fit?
- What would a videotape of my interview say about me?

Downloadable TOOL 2.1

Negotiating Prep and Guidelines*

(For each dimension)

My opening:_____

My expected:_____

My minimum:_____

My walkaway:_____

Their walkaway:_____

Their maximum:_____

Their expected:_____

Their opening:_____

Get Started

Somehow, negotiations are always easier if you can start by agreeing. Find the areas that you agree on and discuss them first.

Areas of agreement:

_____

_____

_____

_____

_____

_____

Areas for Debate

There's a framework for areas where there's a difference as well:

State your position.

Support your position with other information.

Listen to the other person's position and probe for understanding. Don't challenge at this point. Just seek to understand.
Areas for debate:

_____

_____

_____

_____

_____

_____

Find Alternatives

Look for ways to meet everyone's needs. Often this involves bringing another dimension into the picture.

_____

_____

Gain Agreement

Again, there's a process for managing this:
Receive and make proposals.

_____

_____

Receive and make concessions on different dimensions.

_____

_____

Summarize the situation.

_____

_____

Test agreements.

_____

_____

Circle back to concessions until there is complete agreement.

_____

_____

Implement

Implementing is all about following through. You need to do what you say you're going to do. You need to communicate steps along the way. You need to deliver. You need to monitor all the parties so you know they are delivering as well.

CHAPTER 3

Map and *Avoid* the Most Common Land Mines

Part I—**POSITION** and **SELL** yourself; **MAP** and **AVOID** land mines; Do your **DUE DILIGENCE**

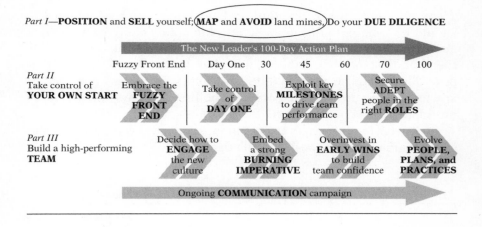

I n some parts of our world, land mines are everywhere. Their prevalence can be attributed to the facts that they are easy to create, are seldom detected, and can cause significant damage and surprise when eventually triggered. In August 2005, *BusinessWeek* magazine reported that there is great hope in using bees to detect these land mines by conditioning the bees to associate the explosive chemicals of land mines with food, thereby providing a safe way to indicate where land mines may be buried. Who would have thought that simple bees would lend hope to defeating such a horrible explosive weapon?

The first 100 days of an executive's transition are also rife with land mines; and just like the real thing, they are usually hidden and are often undetected until it is too late. The awareness that land mines exist is a key factor in limiting their devastating potential.

This chapter provides a map showing where those onboarding land mines might occur, how they are created, and most importantly, when they are most likely to exist. Embedded in our 100-Day Plan is a land mine deactivation methodology. Each step suggested in our 100-Day Plan has taken into account the most common derailing land mines that executives create.

The Dangerous Seven

There are seven major onboarding land mines, each of which you should be looking to dismantle at specific points along your journey. You cannot reduce the risks inherent in a new role until you identify them, understand their danger, and either dance around them or purposefully deactivate them. While land mines can be encountered at any time, there are specific points in the first 100 days when you are most likely to encounter them.

Chart 3.1 summarizes the seven most dangerous land mines and indicates the best time to deactivate them.

CHART 3.1   Top Seven Onboarding Land Mines

	Land Mines	Description	Best Stage to Mitigate/Deactivate
1	Organization	Lack of a winning strategy or the inability to implement that strategy	Before accepting job
2	Role	Expectations and resources or key stakeholders are not aligned	Before accepting job
3	Personal	Gaps exist in the executive's strengths, motivation, or fit	Before accepting job
4	Relationship	Failure to build or maintain key relationships, up, across, or down	Fuzzy front end
5	Learning	Failure to gain adequate information, awareness, or knowledge of customers, collaborators, capabilities, competitors, or conditions	Fuzzy front end
6	Delivery	Failure to build a high-performing team or deliver results fast enough	First 100 days
7	Adjustment	Failure to see or react to situational changes	As appropriate

Chart 3.1 shows that much of the mitigation and deactivation of the most common onboarding land mines is best started early in the process. This is critical information, as most executives do not even begin to recognize or mitigate potential land mines until days or weeks after they have been on the job. Just by being aware of the mines and by working to avoid them early on, you'll significantly increase your chances of avoiding the failure trap.

WARNING!

We are going to talk about these land mines one by one; but they frequently come in multiples and often interact with each other. Exposure to one risk heightens others, and failure has a way of gaining its own terrible and often unstoppable momentum.

Land Mine 1: *Organization*

Organizational land mines are encountered when an executive accepts a new role in an organization that lacks a clear, concise, differentiating and winning strategy. An organization may even have a solid strategic plan but cannot implement it or may offer few or no backup choices should the original plan require putting the executive in a risky predicament.

The best way to avoid this land mine is by making a powerful and fully informed choice, early on. It is important to make sure that it is a choice, that you know what you're getting into, and that you are not joining an organization that is in trouble without knowing it. Be careful not to make the mistake of letting the excitement of the new job, bigger paycheck, or better title overpower your reasoning skills. You do not want to get on a ship that has already sunk. Some people thrive on this risk and want to be part of the turnaround. It is one thing to be a turnaround expert going into an organization that knows it needs to make significant changes fast. It is a recipe for disaster if you are not a turnaround expert and you're going into an organization that needs those skills.

If you are afraid to ask the tough questions that will give you a true read on the organization that you are about to enter, then buyer beware. (You'll find more on asking those tough questions and ways to mitigate organizational land mines in Chapter 4.)

Louisa had been looking for a job for 18 months. She took a job with a growing division of a major player in the software business. They were trying to expand into a completely new area and asked her to come in as VP of marketing for the new group. She had been lobbying for the general manager role, but settled for the marketing job because she was so excited about the new division's prospects. She should not have been.

As it turned out, the division had no competitive advantage and was competing against an entrenched competitor that had quickly stepped into the gap on which Louisa's new company had staked the division's future. Six months into the job, Louisa recommended the company abandon the effort and focus its efforts on other things. It was the right recommendation for the organization, but bad for Louisa as she was out of a job again.

Land Mine 2: *Role*

Role land mines are encountered when expectations, resources, or key stakeholders are not aligned. Often executives step into jobs that are virtually impossible from the start because the expectations that exist are unrealistic or cannot be delivered for whatever reason. The most common indication of role land mines is when key stakeholders are not aligned around the new executive's (1) role and responsibilities, (2) deliverables, (3) authority, (4) interactions, and (5) access to essential resources. It is critical for new leaders to know *exactly* what their boss expects them to deliver and what resources can be controlled and influenced to deliver against those expectations.

One new president had done a great job of negotiating his title and package, but had failed to consider reporting lines and resources. He soon learned that neither the heads of marketing, finance, information, nor human resources reported to him. His only direct reports were the heads of sales and business development. By taking the title of "President," without the appropriate authority, all he had managed to do was to paint a target on his back for his peers to shoot at so they could get him out of the way and strengthen their own positions.

Land Mine 3: *Personal*

Personal land mines are the ones that the executive brings to the new job. They are activated when significant gaps exist in an executive's strengths, motivation, or fit for the job. Often executives assume that their strengths are well matched to a particular role, when in fact they are not. Assumptions about strengths are usually based on prior success without a true in-depth evaluation of strengths. Although a new job may sound like the executive's former job, there will be a whole new set of dynamics that may require significantly different skill sets. By missing this factor, leaders often fail to realize that they may not possess certain strengths that are essential for success in the new role.

After years of working at large consumer product companies, Alice moved to Santa Monica, California, to join a start-up social networking site as the chief marketing officer. She was excited to be moving into a "hot new company," and she was thrilled with her promotion in title. Alice was hired to bring her experience in traditional marketing to the start-up. On her first day in the job, she called the marketing team together to ask for the market research studies, the most recent membership feedback, focus group results, brand positioning strategy, and the current marketing strategy and category spend. She was shocked that none of that existed in the typical format and depth that she had grown accustomed to, if at all.

Alice knew that she had to make quick decisions on some key marketing areas, but she had no idea how to do that without her traditional tools or how to motivate a staff that was far different from the traditional marketing staff that she had worked with in the past. She struggled with the entrepreneurial environment and discovered that just being an expert in brand management was not enough to survive in a fast-paced start-up. She struggled in almost everything she did and soon realized that the hot new company was not a fit for her motivations or her strengths. "I had the marketing skills, but I did not have any clue about the skills required in a start-up environment."

Land Mine 4: *Relationship*

Relationship land mines are most likely to occur when an executive fails to identify, establish, or maintain key relationships up, across, or down. These key relationships are those that have a stake in or can impact the executive's success, we refer to these people as "stakeholders" and they can be found up, down, or across the organization from the new leader. This part of the onboarding journey is often the most densely populated with potential land mines. When an executive misses the needs or agendas of other key stakeholders or outside influencers, there is a good chance that some impact will be felt. If an executive lends an insufficient or ineffective effort to building a productive teamwork environment with direct reports, land mines are often the result. If expectations of up stakeholders are not clearly understood, go unchecked, or frequently change, this is certainly dangerous territory for land mines. Finally, poor preparation and communication follow-through are often key culprits in activating relationship land mines.

Relationship land mines catch many executives. These are especially tricky because sometimes the results of stepping on one do not show up for months, or longer. What is worse, you can get caught by these land mines just by pure neglect of a key stakeholder or someone that you didn't even know should be a key stakeholder.

Relationship risks are particularly severe for people who are brought in as change agents. Often those people come in with a hero mentality, thinking they are the organization's savior. This is not always a problem because sometimes they're right. The problem occurs when new leaders *act* as if they are saviors. Nobody wants to see that, especially those who have been part of the situation that needs saving. It is impossible to act like a savior and be a team leader at the same time. You have to choose one or the other. Always choose the latter. The world is littered with many dead heroes who never made it home.

Sebastian came into the organization to create a new ventures group. He mapped most of the key stakeholders and was building relationships with them. After a while, it became apparent that Suri, the head of another division, was undermining his efforts. Sebastian did not understand why, since he had never come in contact with Suri.

Eventually, Sebastian learned that Suri was upset that he had not seen her as important enough to establish a relationship with early on. She watched as he built relationships all around her and left her out. She felt he was purposely snubbing her. Suri was upset, not because of something Sebastian had done or said, but because he had not said anything to her at all. Her efforts to undermine him were an immature way of showing her disappointment, but she wanted him to know that she could make things difficult for him. Sebastian overlooked her when he built his key stakeholder list and it cost him months later.

Land Mine 5: *Learning*

Executives trigger learning land mines when they fail to grasp key information in any of the so-called *5Cs:* Customers, Collaborators,

Capabilities, Competitors, or Conditions. Often executives miss the importance of certain Cs or diminish the importance of one or more. If an executive doesn't have a learning plan in place for *each* and *every* C, the likelihood of land mines increases.

If leaders don't know what they need to know, or worse yet, don't know what they don't know, then land mines will surely be plentiful. So what do leaders need to know? At the very least, the leader needs to know critical information about each of the 5Cs, especially about the real value chain of their business. If you use our guidelines for your 5C analysis (see Appendix II), the information you gather will significantly diminish the risk of learning land mines.

Truly, learning is essential. Being perceived as wanting to learn is almost as important as learning itself. You have heard it before: "Seek first to understand,"[1] "don't come in with the answer,"[2] "wisdom begins in wonder."[3] You hear it repeatedly in many different ways, because it is proven advice. Heed it. You need to learn and you'll want to be perceived as being hungry to learn.

Harold joined a company that was helping companies take advantage of favorable tax treatments for new technologies. He had done his homework well across the most of the 5Cs. He liked the team. They liked him. He knew exactly how he could add value to the group and to its customers. What he had failed to learn about was that the government was about to change the law and take away the favorable tax treatments. So, a few months into the job, the company effectively got legislated out of business.

Land Mine 6: *Delivery*

In the end, it boils down to delivery. It's not what you do; it's the results you deliver. Strategies and plans always work on PowerPoint presentations, but they often fail to work when they meet reality. If you get everything else right but fail to deliver, you will fail. If you deliver, the organization can tolerate many other faults. If you are a sole practitioner, you can perhaps deliver through your own sheer

---

[1]Steven Covey, *The 7 Habits of Highly Effective People* (New York: Simon & Schuster, 1989).
[2]Michael Watkins, *The First 90 Days* (Watertown, MA: Harvard Business School Press, 2003).
[3]Attributed to Socrates.

effort. However, if you are leading a team, you cannot deliver if the team does not deliver. At the end of your first 100 days, the most dangerous land mine is failing to build a high-performance team fast enough to deliver the expected results in the expected time frame.

To be clear, this is about real delivery. It is not about manipulating expectations to get the base low. It is not about picking the wrong battles. It is not even about the process to get there. It is about putting points on the board with real impact. Delivery comes in all forms, but it is only valuable if it is what was ordered. It's easy. Know what's expected. Validate what's expected. Deliver what's expected. Do that, and you've won.

Steve was hired as the head of business development for a venture-backed technology company that had developed a cutting edge digital rights management (DRM) software. Steve was excited about the opportunity because he knew that the technology was one of the best and the market was screaming for such a DRM product that was easy and reliable to use. Steve's main priority was to enter into long-term agreements with the major entertainment studios.

Steve made inroads with the studios quickly but he became frustrated by their notoriously slow movement. While keeping his eye on the studio business, he began to concentrate on other industries that required DRM technology and was able to secure a strong deal flow.

A year later Steve was fired after a meeting with the venture capital company. Although Steve was pleased with his inroads at the studios, he had not yet closed any deals with a major entertainment firm. Whereas he felt the deal flow from other industries compensated, he didn't understand that his up stakeholders thought he was concentrating 100 percent on studio business and felt that that business was far more valuable than the other industries that Steve had mined. He delivered, but he delivered off strategy.

Land Mine 7: *Adjustment*

Executives can do everything correctly to this point, but if they do not see or react to the inevitable situational changes, then new land mines will certainly be created. The act of planning and managing is not a static exercise and the executive must be keenly aware of the fluid nature of all the dynamics of the team's situation. Missing the need to constantly survey the environment and adjust accordingly is just like a skipper setting sail for a destination and never adjusting his sails for the ever-changing seas and weather conditions.

Things change and you need to change when they do. Sometimes you can get away with minor adjustments. Sometimes a complete restart is required. The risk lies in not seeing the need to change or in being too slow to react to the changes you do see.

Tony was hired by Victor to run the operations of the division that Victor headed. Tony reported directly to Victor and soon after joining, he realized that the division was significantly underperforming. Tony embraced the challenge and made great gains in operational efficiencies in a short time; but while operations were improving, other aspects of the division continued to falter. As a result, Wendy, one of Victor's counterparts from a sister division was promoted to head both divisions. So now, Tony was reporting to Victor who was now reporting to Wendy. Tony thought that this move represented no big change for him.

He was wrong. He was sure that Victor would represent his work to Wendy and he had assumed his style and approach would be embraced because it was producing results. What he did not know is that Wendy's division had been run under a completely different operational style and her division's results were far stronger than Victor's ever had been.

For Tony, the change was huge, which usually indicates that a huge adjustment is also required. Tony missed the "huge change" part, and therefore it never crossed his mind that a "huge adjustment" might be required. Any change in structure requires another look at what is going on, if not a complete restart. Tony did not do that. He kept soldiering on, assuming that Victor would make his case to Wendy.

Two months later Victor and everyone he had brought in to work for him, including Tony, were fired.

Map and *Avoid* the Most Common Land Mines—Summary and Implications

There are seven dangerous onboarding risks: Organization, Role, Personal Skills, Learning, Relationship, Delivery, and Adjustment.

Almost every one of these land mines is either created or reactivated by actions or inactions of the executive. So, in essence executives are in almost complete control of how many land mines they may create, reactivate, or detonate along the way.

Be aware that the mitigation of land mines begins far sooner than most executives think. Your land mine deactivation approach is important and must start early:

> *Phase 1—The offer-to-acceptance stage:* Uncover and manage Organization, Role, and Personal land mines before accepting the job.
>
> *Phase 2—The acceptance-to-start stage:* Learning what you need to know and use the 5Cs as your guideline. Learning early is essential. Be sure to jump-start your relationships as early as you can. Keep close attention to up, down, and across stakeholders. Be careful not to miss anyone who can have an impact on your career.
>
> *Phase 3—The after-the-start and always stage:* Build a high-performing team to execute and deliver. Keep an eye on the landscape and adjust as needed.

Inevitably, no matter how good of a deactivator you are, you will step on a land mine at some point. The goal is to avoid as many as you can and be in a position to react decisively when you detonate one. When a land mine rears its ugly head, keep yours and hit the restart button. Who needs bees?

CHAPTER 4

Do Your *Due Diligence* on the Organization, Role, and Fit

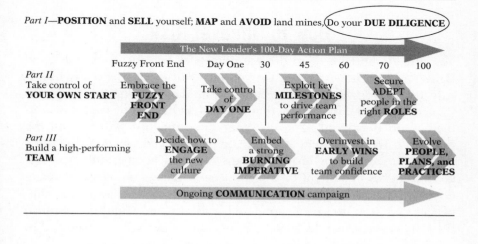

Part I—**POSITION** and **SELL** yourself; **MAP** and **AVOID** land mines, (Do your **DUE DILIGENCE**)

The New Leader's 100-Day Action Plan

Fuzzy Front End · Day One · 30 · 45 · 60 · 70 · 100

Part II
Take control of
YOUR OWN START · Embrace the **FUZZY FRONT END** · Take control of **DAY ONE** · Exploit key **MILESTONES** to drive team performance · Secure **ADEPT** people in the right **ROLES**

Part III
Build a high-performing
TEAM · Decide how to **ENGAGE** the new culture · Embed a strong **BURNING IMPERATIVE** · Overinvest in **EARLY WINS** to build team confidence · Evolve **PEOPLE, PLANS, and PRACTICES**

Ongoing **COMMUNICATION** campaign

I wish I'd read this chapter before I accepted that job!"

We hear that a lot.

Almost nobody wants to do due diligence. Almost nobody likes to do due diligence. Almost nobody knows how to do due diligence well. It's as though people don't want to do anything to spoil the moment of getting a job offer and knowing that somebody else appreciates them. Ignorance can be bliss . . . until the things you didn't see, show up and sting you on the head.

It won't surprise you to learn that we think due diligence is important. But then, we also think it's a good idea to look both ways before crossing a busy street, and that it's a good idea to check for barely submerged rocks before diving into a lake.

In this chapter, we suggest that you figure out organizational, role, and personal risks during due diligence. We suggest a process for doing that. We also suggest a framework for dealing with those risks once you've figured them out. You may want to follow our suggestions. Or later you can send us an e-mail saying "I wish I'd read this chapter before I accepted that job!" You won't be alone.

Another advantage of doing due diligence is that it can be a good way to open communication channels that may be mutually valuable down the road. We have much more on communication later in the book.

How to Uncover Risk

You already know how to do due diligence. You just may not know that you know how to do it. Or, you may not think it is really necessary. Or you may be uncomfortable asking the tough questions. Know that it is essential and know that it is not as painful or time consuming as you may think. You use your due diligence skill sets all the time. It is the same skill set that you've deployed when you've done situation analyses for business plans or hired people and done reference checks or bought cars or houses or picked a college or made decisions based on incomplete information. At the core, due diligence is an exercise in collecting and analyzing information to reduce the risk inherent in a decision. Like just about everything discussed in this book, a carefully thought out and methodical approach will help. We suggest three steps:

1. Decide what information to collect.
2. Identify potential sources of information.
3. Gather and analyze the information.

We have combined gathering and analyzing because they are iterative. Your analysis will help you decide how much more information you need.

Decide What Information to Collect

To avoid trying to boil the ocean, you've got to focus your risk assessment on exploring the few most important areas. Before accepting a job, you must gather information in the following areas to answer three fundamental questions around organization, role, and personal risks. The Due Diligence Checklist at the end of this chapter (Tool 4.1) can help you keep track of these.

Organizational Risk: What Is the Organization's Sustainable Competitive Advantage?

When looking at Organizational Risk, be sure to assess risk elements across Customers, Collaborators, Capabilities, Competitors, and Conditions. The good news is that you probably have a significant head start on understanding many of these or you wouldn't even have been considered for the job. But do not rely on what you think you know. Go through the exercise and see what new things you can learn. In particular, you need to understand all these in the light of the specific job you've been offered. Here are some headlines about the 5Cs. See Appendix II, "Situational Assessment," for a more detailed explanation and useful worksheets.

The 5Cs

1. *Customers:* First line, customer chain, end users, influencers
2. *Collaborators:* Suppliers, allies, government/community leaders
3. *Capabilities:* Human, operational, financial, technical, key assets
4. *Competitors:* Direct, indirect, potential
5. *Conditions:* Social/demographic, political/government/regulatory, economic, market

Role Risk: Did Anyone Have Concerns about This Role; and, If so, What Was Done to Mitigate Them?

To mitigate this risk, you should:

1. Find the people who had concerns.
2. Understand those concerns.
3. Understand what has changed to make those concerns go away.
4. Believe that those people will support the role (and you) going forward.

This may require some iterative conversations. Most likely, somebody had concerns. Almost certainly, somebody internally wanted the job or part of the job. There is always somebody who wanted things realigned in a different way. You should find those people and understand their concerns. Then, you need to know *if* and *how* they were made to feel better. Knowing who is *not* onboard with your new role is often as important as knowing who is onboard.

You should also know and understand a few of things about the role itself before accepting the job:

- Why does the position exist? Why did they need to create it in the first place?
- What are the objectives and outcomes? What are you supposed to get done?
- What will the impact be on the rest of the organization? What kind of interactions can you expect with key stakeholders?
- What are your specific responsibilities, including decision-making authority and direct reports?

The fundamental issue here has to do with making sure the key stakeholders are aligned around the role's reason to exist, objectives, impact, responsibilities, and interdependencies with each other.

Personal Risk: What, Specifically, about Me, Led to You Offering Me the Job?
The basic questions are:

- Is this the company and role that can best capitalize on your strengths over time?
- Will you look forward to coming to work there three weeks, months, or years from now?
- Will you fit with the culture?

The goal is to find out if your strengths, motivation, and fit are a match for what is required to deliver the expected results. Knowing what you know, would you hire yourself for the job? If there are significant differences, probe and explore, and keep the option of walking away open in your mind.

Identify Potential Sources of Information
Many successful and competent people are weak in this skill. First, know yourself on this point. If you are lost, is it really difficult for you

to stop and ask for directions? If so, extend this impulse to your work situation. How good are you at getting information from third-party sources? Many people shut down what they consider "gossip" with the feeling that it is an inefficient use of time and is morally suspect. A lot of it is, to be sure, but the fact is that people like to talk and a lot of what they say is deeply informative about the organization. Even if you feel this way about malicious gossip, some clear-headed thinking about this can help you realize that there is virtuous "gossip," or informal discussion, that is absolutely vital to your ability to understand your environment. You will fail if you underestimate or disregard this fundamental truth.

So, you need to identify sources of information. You'll need scouts, seconds, and spies to help you. Scouts are people outside the company who can give you a view of what's going on inside the company. Seconds are people who want to help you succeed. Spies are people on the inside who can give you special insight into what's going on.

One of the advantages of information gathering is that it can be a good way to start to open mutually valuable communication channels for use down the road. This is where this happens, and these are some of those people with whom you want to have those open channels.

If you cross the 5Cs with scouts, seconds, and spies, you can come up with a pretty good list of potential sources of information. The key word here is "potential." You're not going to talk to everybody on the list. You're not going to gather every possible bit of information. You're going to start with the most important information sources and then iterate between gathering and analyzing until you've satisfied yourself with the answers to the three key questions. With that in mind, Chart 4.1 provides a list of potential sources of information.

Be aware that the first valuable data you get from your information-gathering efforts may be the degree of comfort your new company shows about your search. If the company is open to your learning everything you can before you accept, that is a very good sign. If the company absolutely blocks you from learning anything, be careful.

Your information gathering should likely start by laying out your due diligence plan with the person(s) who offered you the job. Let them know what you want to learn and how you want to do it. Position this along the lines of you're wanting to learn as much as you can before you accept because you're anticipating this being a long-term relationship and you want to make absolutely sure the fit is right.

CHART 4.1   Potential Sources of Information for Uncovering Risks

Areas of Risk	Roles	Sources
Customers	Scouts	Customers and analysts who follow customers or the industry and can provide insight about the organization.
	Seconds	Internal and external mentors and coaches who know customers.
	Spies	People who call on customers from within your new organization.
Collaborators	Scouts	Suppliers, agencies, allies, and analysts who provide insight about the organization by following suppliers, agencies, and allies.
	Seconds	Internal and external mentors and coaches who know suppliers, agencies, and allies.
	Spies	People who work with suppliers and allies within your new organization.
Capabilities	Scouts	People inside the organization, former employees, and analysts following the organization or the industry who can provide insight about capabilities and how things work inside the organization.
	Seconds	Internal and external mentors and coaches who know the organization.
	Spies	People at multiple levels in the organization who can tell you the truth (especially good sources are future direct reports, peers you have not yet met, board members as appropriate, and other key players).
Competitors	Scouts	Customers, suppliers, agencies, allies, and analysts following the competition who can provide insight about competitors.
	Seconds	Internal and external mentors and coaches who know competitors.
	Spies	Be careful here. Even though you have not yet accepted a job with your new organization, the right thing to do is to start behaving as though you are a part of that organization with regard to spying on competitors. Don't do anything you wouldn't want blown up on the front page of the *Wall Street Journal* later.
Conditions	Scouts	Social, demographic, political, government, regulatory, economic experts, and analysts and journalists who cover these areas.
	Seconds	Internal and external mentors and coaches who understand general conditions.
	Spies	People at multiple levels in the organization who can tell you unvarnished truths about the impact of conditions on the organization (especially good sources are future direct reports, peers you have not yet met, board members as appropriate, and other key players).

Gather and Analyze the Information

Gathering information is an art, a skill honed with practice. Like all aspects of communication, some of us are better at it than others. You could identify all the right information to collect, line up all the right sources of information, and then fail miserably at getting what you need if you go about it in the wrong way. If you're lucky, all you need to do is ask and you shall receive. But, as discussed in Chapters 7 and 8, communication is rarely that simple or easy. Trust is the grease that lets communication work and conversely communication is what builds and sustains trust.

Especially when you're new, you need to create "trust effects" quickly and easily. Self-awareness will go a long way here. Are you good at helping people feel comfortable, and do they open up to you? If not, you need to work on this skill. If you are, you still should seek to get better at it as you move up the leadership ladder.

The quickest and most effective tip we can give is that a genuine concern about the organization's ability to succeed will start opening the doors of communication. That coupled with a sensitivity and concern for the person you are seeking information from will further open those doors. If you can portray both of those trust effects, people will *want* to help you. For a lot of leaders, especially new leaders, the Achilles' heel is their own pride and aspiration. If you ask for help or information in a genuine way, people will give it to you and it will actually make them feel good doing so. This is especially true in the information-gathering phase, so take advantage it and don't be afraid to ask for information or help. If you do it correctly, you will gather the information you need, you will make your sources feel good, and you will begin to develop trusting relationships.

What? So What? Now What?

You've gathered your information (what). You've analyzed it and thought about it (so what). Now what do you do? We suggest categorizing the risk as low, manageable, mission-crippling, or insurmountable and then taking appropriate action.

Low Level of Risk

Don't confuse this with a low level of risk *found*. If you've neglected to gather the required information and therefore have either not found risk, or classified it incorrectly as a low risk, then you deserve whatever pain comes your way. If you come away from this effort with the assessment that there is no risk, you probably did a lousy job in your information gathering or you are about to walk into a rare situation.

Why do we say that? Because there are always risks. That's why we are so keen on proper information gathering. If the risk isn't there now, it will show up later. But if the organization has a sustainable competitive advantage for now, and if key people are aligned around a common, clear definition of the role you're going to take, and if you would hire yourself for that role in this organization at this time, you should be in good shape at the start. Go on to Chapter 5. Do the rest of the things we suggest and enjoy the ride. Just keep your eyes open for the inevitable changes and their inherent risks.

Manageable Level of Risk

None of this is an exercise in eliminating risk. It is an exercise in iden-tifying risk so you can manage it. If your efforts uncover a manage-able level of risk, you should feel good for two reasons. First, you've found the risks even before you accepted the job. Second, you're confident you can manage them. This would include the following situations:

- The organization has a competitive advantage, but it's being threatened.
- The organization knows how to create a sustainable competitive advantage, but they haven't locked it in yet.
- The role is clear, but not all are aligned.
- You don't exactly have the strength they thought you did, but you know how to compensate for that gap.

In these situations, go ahead and accept the job and manage these risks as you go.

Mission-Crippling Risk

This is where the fun stops. This is where you've uncovered something that is going to keep you from being successful unless you can change it. The critical judgment in this whole exercise is separating manageable risk from mission-crippling risk. By classifying something as manageable, you are saying you *can* make things work. By classifying something as mission-crippling, you're saying you *cannot* be successful with a change. So before you accept this role, you should be certain that you have the authority and can implement the necessary changes to resolve or mitigate this risk. If not, you should walk away.

If you have not yet accepted the job, you're in a strong negotiating position because you can choose to try to figure out a mitigation plan or walk away. No organization you'd ever want to be a part of wants to set you up for failure. If there's a mission-crippling risk, it is in everyone's best interest to resolve it. Typical mission-critical risks include:

- Lack of resources required for you or the organization to achieve its objectives
- Lack of clarity and alignment on your role and its responsibility and authority vis-à-vis others
- Insufficient support from your team, your boss, or key stakeholders
- Severe conditional changes without a plan to weather the storm

If you're already in the job and discover a mission-crippling risk, things are a little tougher, mostly because it's harder to walk away. This means you'll have a bias to classify things as manageable that may be mission-crippling. As painful as it may be over the short-term, if you cannot succeed without something changing, devote the time and effort to get it changed before you try to move forward.

Insurmountable Barrier
An insurmountable barrier is a mission-crippling risk that cannot (or will not) be resolved. As painful as it is to find these, finding them before you accept the job is dramatically less painful than finding them later. If it feels insurmountable, it is. Listen to your intuition.

HOT TIP

Manageable versus mission-crippling risk: The difference between manageable and mission-crippling risk is a judgment call. Be confident in your own judgment. If you don't think the risk is manageable, it isn't. Change things as quickly as possible. Mitigate the risks or walk away.

Do Your Due Diligence—Summary and Implications

The most opportune time to complete your due diligence is between the offer and acceptance phases. Waiting until later or ignoring this step can be devastating to your potential for success. During this step, you should be making sure the job is right for you. Mitigate organization, role, and personal risks by answering three questions:

1. What is the organization's *sustainable competitive advantage?*
2. Did anyone have *concerns about this role;* and, if so, what was done to mitigate them?
3. *What, specifically, about me,* led to your offering me the job?

In assessing these risks, three steps can help:

1. Decide what information to collect.
2. Identify potential sources of information: Scouts, Seconds, and Spies across Customers, Collaborators, Capabilities, Competitors, and Conditions.
3. Gather and analyze the information.

Then:

If you're facing:	You should:
A low level of risk	Do nothing out of the ordinary (but keep your eyes open for the inevitable changes to come).
Manageable risk	Manage it in the normal course of your job.
Mission-crippling risk	Resolve before accepting the job or mitigate before doing anything else if already in the job.
Insurmountable barriers	Walk away.

QUESTIONS YOU SHOULD ASK YOURSELF

- Is this the right organization and role for me?
- Am I the right person for this organization and role at this point in my career?
- What is my information-gathering approach?
- What are the risks and how can I mitigate them?

Due Diligence Checklist*

Key questions to answer during due diligence:

1. Mitigate Organizational Risk.
   What is the organization's sustainable competitive advantage?

_____

_____

_____

_____

_____

2. Mitigate Personal Risk.
   What about me, specifically, led to this job offer?

_____

_____

_____

_____

_____

3. Mitigate Role Risk.
   Did anyone have concerns about this role; and, if so, what was done to mitigate them?

_____

_____

_____

_____

_____

(continued)

Downloadable TOOL 4.1   (continued)

Overall Risk Assessment

If You Are Facing	You Should
A low level of risk	Do nothing out of the ordinary (but keep your eyes open for inevitable changes).
Manageable risk	Manage it in the normal course of your job.
Mission-crippling risk	Resolve before accepting the job or mitigate before doing anything else, if you are already in the job.
Insurmountable barriers	Walk away.

CHAPTER 5

Act Differently When You Are *Promoted* from Within

Part I—**POSITION** and **SELL** yourself; **MAP** and **AVOID** land mines, Do your **DUE DILIGENCE**

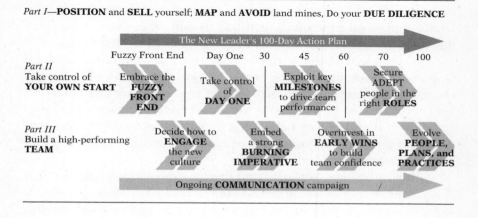

onsider a successful handoff in a running relay race. The new runner, who is already on the track, does three things: (1) prepares and starts moving in advance; (2) takes control of the transition by putting his hand where he wants the baton placed; (3) accelerates decisively following the handoff. Those promoted from within should follow the same model.

The basics of new leadership apply whether it is in a new company or the same company. The fundamental difference between moving to a new company and getting promoted from within is that, like a relay runner preparing to receive the baton, you are already on the track. Unlike when you join an organization for the first time and have to create a new positioning for yourself, when you're promoted from within, people already know you or know people who know you. Thus, to a large degree, this is an exercise in repositioning yourself within the organization.

When you have been promoted from within, keep the following rules in mind.

You Cannot Control the Context

While you may not be able to influence the circumstances surrounding an open role, you often can influence planned promotions in advance. Under a planned promotion, you will usually have time to do some due diligence and transition planning before you are officially named.

When a promotion is unplanned, you must figure out the real story before jumping into the new role. Don't be caught off guard by the surprise of the promotion and forget to do your required due diligence. For you to be successful, you must have some level of understanding of the true story behind the unplanned promotion. The story may be a positive one, or it may be ripe with controversy, but either way, you must know.

Finally, be sure to clarify and deliver expectations whether it is a permanent role or an interim appointment. Determining delivery expectations in a permanent role is an easier process, but interim roles can be tricky because delivery expectations can be all over the map and often are contradictory. If an interim transition is to be successful there must be agreement across the key stakeholders on expected results and time frames.

It Is Hard to Make a Clean Break

In many ways, you are in the new job at the moment of the announcement regardless of what may be announced as your official start date. Unlike coming in from the outside, people know you and can instantly start thinking or imagining you in that role. You may even start to get calls regarding issues and decisions related to the role. Even with these new demands coming at you before you've officially started, you are still accountable for results in your old job.

More often than not, you will still be accountable for your old job even after you start your new job. Going back to the relay-runner analogy, you're really making two handoffs at the same time: the baton you're picking up from the person who had your new job before you and the baton you're handing off to the person taking your old job. With regard to your old job, you don't want to be in a position where you hand the baton over too quickly, too roughly, or not in the place it was requested.

If you falter with the transition of your old job, the results can impinge on your success in your new role. As you reset your stakeholder list for your new role, also keep in mind that you now have an extra set of stakeholders—those who contributed to your success along the way. They will not want to see you flub the transition after helping position you for your new role.

There Is No Honeymoon

As an insider, you're expected to be fully up to speed the moment you start your new job. The good news is that you already have an internal network that you can begin to leverage immediately after your new role is announced. While a promotion is certainly good news, remember that in addition to your supporters, you'll most likely have detractors as well. You'll want to identify them early and keep them on your stakeholder list.

All this leads to three indicated actions for those promoted from within:

1. *Prepare in advance.* Work to understand the context and complexity of the new situation. Get yourself ready and exert whatever influence you can to shape your new role and set up success—as far in advance as possible.

2. *Take control of your own transition. Be proactive* and control the message and communication cascade—the timing of who hears what, in what order—as well as clarifying what has changed and what has not changed. Protect your base by ensuring ongoing positive results in your old job and recognizing those who have helped you along the way.

3. *Accelerate team progress after the start.* This is where your knowledge of the organization can really help you. You and your new team can *get a running start*, leveraging positive momentum to accelerate the key strategic, operational, and organizational processes.

Prepare in Advance

The context of your promotion will affect the early leadership challenges you face. The smoothest and easiest transitions follow planned promotions. When succession planning works and the right leader is in the right spot at the right time, most feel in control and few feel threatened. When this happens to you, be grateful and make the best of a good situation.

But it's not always like that. When there's a sudden leadership gap and you get an unexpected call to fill it, regaining control of the situation and of the rampant runaway emotions can be a significant challenge. Uncertainty is scary for all.

Work to understand the thinking behind the decision and begin communicating with and understanding your new stakeholders. Look carefully at the number and quality of things changing in your own situation. You'll need far more help if you're getting promoted to run a new function in a new industry in a new country than if you're taking over from the boss whose deputy you've been for the past decade. An internal promotion suggests that senior management sees value in continuity, "insider knowledge," and a "known entity" (you) rather than the risk, hassle, and ramp-up time of an outsider. There may be an expectation of change, however, and insiders often lose grip of their opportunity by being afraid to rock the boat. Get a clear sense of the expectations and deliver accordingly.

Perhaps the most challenging case is when you have to fill a gap as the interim leader. It helps a lot to get clarity on whether "interim" means "holding the fort until we find the right person, which absolutely will not be you," or "on probation with a good chance of becoming permanent," or "filling the role on a temporary basis as a developmental opportunity." In either case, it's likely a good posture to engage fully with the work while eschewing the perks of the job—basically focusing your efforts on the least prestigious, highest-impact tasks and leaving the glory to others.

Manage Right through the Interim

Patty had delivered in every job she'd had at the firm for 15 years. When her boss was moved to head a different division, senior management asked her to step in as interim division president while they did a thorough internal and external search for the new president.

Patty kept doing exactly what she'd been doing. She finished the year's strategic planning and got senior management excited about her plans. She kept managing operations—and delivering her numbers. She kept moving ahead with the organizational evolution she and her previous boss had put in place, inspiring and enabling all. In the end, senior management would have looked silly picking anyone but her for the role.

Whatever the context, pause for a moment to craft a solid transition plan that includes identifying key stakeholders and getting clear on your message. Then, get ahead, in particular, by jump-starting relationships with key stakeholders.

Take Control of Your Own Transition

Since you will be perceived as starting your new job at the moment of the announcement, try to control the timing of that announcement especially if you're moving into a vacant position. Remember the announcement process includes far more than just the formal announcement. There are almost always leaks in advance and there are always people who should be told in advance, so you must be careful about the cascade of information. In many cases, you have to manage this down to a minute-by-minute level of detail to make sure people hear about the promotion in the right order, in the right way, from the right person.

This is not a trivial issue. Be particularly sensitive to when, how, and from whom people hear. Emotions will probably be running high and those hearing about the transition may include those who:

- Are being moved out of a job
- Have allies or friends being moved out of a job
- See someone else is getting a role they might have wanted
- See this transition as particularly important to their own success—especially direct reports to and peers of the new role

If you're tempted to simply make one general and official announcement, think again. Trust and relationship building start with how people receive this kind of information. On the one hand, anybody who gets a special advance notice will feel special, and as a new leader, you want to use that capital wisely. On the other hand, it's likely to be impossible for you to do all the one-on-one announcement meetings that you'd like. Even if you could, by the time you made your third or forth announcement, the others on your list would probably have already heard. Also, in many cases, you will want somebody else to relay the information framing the message in the context of their specific role or reporting situation. It is worth thinking all this through and then designing a communication campaign that simply and effectively reaches your key stakeholders.

Start by understanding that there are no secrets. It's not so much that the people you trust with secrets intentionally pass them on, but that they inadvertently slip. An HR executive asked one of us how people always seemed to find out about promotions in advance.

"It's easy. A senior HR person (like you) walks into our general manager's office carrying their big personnel ring binder. People take a guess and then go to that HR executive's assistant and say 'Great news about Larry. Isn't it?' Nine times out of ten, the HR assistant comes back with something along the lines of 'It is.' or 'Larry? Don't you mean Doug?' Either way, they will figure it out."

You can't possibly anticipate and prevent all the ways information is going to leak. Just assume it will and guide the cascade of leaks as much as you can.

Expect Leaks and Manage Them—In Advance

Betty was announcing a set of changes in her organization all at the same time. She wanted to let people know in the right order, make sure they all had the same understanding and not disenfranchise her managers. The key pieces of her announcement cascade included:

- Have one-on-one conversations with individuals most emotionally impacted including key peers, but not external stakeholders, on Tuesday afternoon.
- Place conference call with direct reports at the end of day Tuesday.
  - Allow the evening for them to leak the news to their direct reports.
- Place conference call with her direct reports' direct reports first thing Wednesday.
  - Allow the morning for them to leak the news to their teams.

- Make formal e-mail announcement at 11:55 AM on Wednesday.
- Place all-hands conference call at noon Wednesday to explain changes.

What was effective about Betty's approach was that she built in time for a round of conversations to take place, but didn't let more than a few hours go by without following up. By the time the official announcement happened, all the key parties had been briefed and therefore felt "in the know." For everybody, it felt like "things were under control." And they were.

Different Transitions Require Different Tactics

Gena was announcing a set of changes to her organization. She was promoting one person to lead manufacturing and announcing that the current head of quality control was leaving within the next six months and that his replacement was to be named later. Gena wanted to calm the direct reports of the exiting quality control leader preemptively without disempowering the newly named manufacturing leader. So, here's what she did:

- With regard to those people whose boss was going to be replaced within six months, she called each of them one-on-one just before the formal announcement to urge them to communicate any issues directly with her during the transition period.
- With regard to those people whose new boss was being named in the announcement, she did no preannouncement calls but left it to the new leader to call each of his direct reports individually immediately after the announcement (but not before).

Here again, Gena was tactically very shrewd. She helped channel potential disgruntlement to herself, while allowing the head of manufacturing to establish his authority.

Announcement Cascade Time Line

Tool 5.1 at the end of this chapter is an announcement cascade checklist. Let's walk through the key components of stakeholders, message, preannouncement, formal announcement, and postannouncement.

Stakeholders

Start with mapping and prioritizing the internal and external stakeholders.

Internal stakeholders might include:

- Former peers who helped you and your team get to the point where you deserve this new move
- New peers who are going to help you and your team be successful in advance
- Other people in your informal network inside the company—no matter what their level or official role—who can help you or your team learn and get things done (perhaps including the incumbent under the right circumstances)
- Former and new team members

External stakeholders might include:

- Key customers—particularly those with close relationships with people involved in the changes
- Key suppliers and analysts
- Community leaders, government officials, regulators, and the like

Message

The platform for change, vision, and call to action here aren't any different from those you'd use when coming in from the outside. The point is to clarify them before you do anything else.

Preannouncement Time Line

Map the order in which you're going to tell people in advance, understanding that the more people you tell and the further in advance, the greater the number of leaks there will be.

Formal Announcement

This is the formal mass communication that goes out. Be clear on what it says, who says it, and exactly when it's distributed. This will influence your postannouncement time line.

Postannouncement Time Line

Now that the cat's out of the bag, you don't have to worry about leaks anymore, but you do need to control the order of the communications.

You can do this by using a combination of mass, large group, small group, and one-on-one sessions to get your message out to the people you need to reach in a time frame that supports your announcement objectives.

"Presume Not That I Am the Thing I Was"[1]

After the announcement of your promotion, be as clear as you can be about what is changed and what is the same. People will be trying to figure out the new you as quickly as they can. Everything you say and don't say or do and don't do will be interpreted and misinterpreted by someone.

"Everyone" includes those staying behind in your old world. In some cases, you'll be asked to continue to manage your old role during the transition. In others, someone else will pick it up. But in all cases, the positive or negative results in your old job will affect people's perceptions of you. This is why you must protect your base, ideally by making sure you've got someone ready to fill your old role and working with the person to support a smooth transition. Your replacement's success is your success.

Know That It Is Hard to Make a Clean Break

Jean had recently taken over the company's operations in one country and had gotten off to a particularly fast start. Her management was so impressed that they quickly promoted her again to take on a global operation. Unfortunately, the team in the country she had been running was not yet strong enough to continue to be successful without Jean's leadership. There was no replacement for Jean in sight. Jean had not prepared for another promotion that fast, and failed to control the transition. She kept getting dragged back to fix things in her "old" country and couldn't give her new role and team the attention they so desperately needed to accelerate progress. Not surprisingly, this story did not have a happy ending as people in both her old and new areas started doubting Jean's leadership.

Be Prepared to Enlist Support to Make a Fast Start

When Pat's management decided to merge another division in with hers, she immediately pulled together a group to help map out and

---

[1]Shakespeare's newly crowned Henry V in *Henry IV*, act V, scene v: "Presume not that I am the thing I was; For God doth know, so shall the world perceive, That I have turn'd away my former self."

implement the transition, including figuring out which people would best fill the new, combined roles. Pat and the group managed the timing of the communications so people heard about the changes in the way Pat chose, through a combination of e-mails, videos, large and small group meetings, one-on-one phone calls, and live conversations. All this contributed to a smooth transition for Pat and thus her team's success in the new combined division.

HOT TIP

Strive to shorten the time between announcement and start: One of the biggest differences between joining from the outside and getting promoted from within is that more time between announcement and start is better when joining from the outside to give you time for preparation and preboarding conversations. When you are promoted from within, less time between announcement and start is better to minimize the period when you're doing two jobs.

Accelerate Team Progress after the Start

Many executives promoted from the inside underestimate how quickly the organization will change their perception about them and how quickly and naturally a new pecking order takes place. Most people are simply practical about this kind of change. "Well, Ron's the boss now. Let's figure out how he wants these things done and do it that way." Be aware, however, that not everybody is so pragmatic and accepting. Inside knowledge goes two ways. Your network includes supporters and detractors. Some of those detractors are people you rubbed the wrong way in previous roles, others will be created during this transition. Watch out for those who wanted all or part of your new job and be prepared for some people to work against your success. As Sun-Tzu says, "Keep your friends close, and your enemies closer." [2]

Some of this is, perhaps, inevitable. Make sure your supporters, scouts, and seconds keep you aware of the mood of the large group, observe what any detractors might be doing or saying, and counter

---

[2] This was originally said by Sun-Tzu ~400 BC, despite most of us remembering it as one of the maxims Michael Corleone's father taught him "here in this room," in the film *The Godfather II.*

negativity as much as is practical. This is important, but don't get overinvested in this. Your goal is to create positive momentum quickly, and then turn your attention to accelerating progress by evolving the three critical processes: strategic, operational, and organizational.

Tackle the strategies first. Be mindful of the difference between stated strategies (what's on paper) and the de facto strategy (what's really being implemented). They don't always match. If the Burning Imperative is not in place or not really shared, you have to do that first.

Once you've got strategies going in the right direction, move on to the operational practices. This is about turning theoretical strategies into things that actually happen by ensuring disciplined execution of the action plans. Disciplined execution is all about running the plan, conducting milestone meetings as a *team*.

The third thing to do is to ensure capabilities grow in sync with operational needs. In Chapter 13, we present different ideas geared to getting ADEPT (an acronym for Acquisition, Development, Encouragement, Planning, and Transitioning) people in the right roles with the right support over time and revolving around talent.

Make It Real

Soon after Tom's promotion, he met with his key people for a day to dig into their thinking and recalibrate what was important. At the end of the day, he told the team he agreed with their stated strategies but felt that they had not been given the resources they needed to make them real. Tom took the case to management to increase the group's budget to properly seed the new initiatives. The plan was so compelling that he won the additional resources. So he doubled the advertising spending against the existing campaign, quadrupled the funding for marketing efforts geared to professional recommenders, and quintupled the public relations budget. Over the next two years, Tom and his team grew the business a combined 50 percent.

Adjusting to a New Boss[3]

Sometimes in interim roles, you'll have an overlap with the person replacing you at the back end. Even though that's a relatively short period inside an interim assignment, take it seriously. It doesn't

---

[3] This was adapted from Coyne and Coyne's article, "Surviving Your New CEO," *Harvard Business Review*, May 2007, and then expanded.

matter how successful you and your team have been. It doesn't matter what your previous results and ratings were. Whether it's interim or permanent, a new boss reshuffles the deck, just as you do when you're the new boss. Given that, here are some tips for adjusting to a new boss under any circumstances:

- *Foundation:* Treat your new boss decently as a human being; make the boss feel welcome, valued, and valuable. Enable the new boss to do good work. Do your job well—and not the boss's.

- *Attitude:* Choose to be optimistic. Believe the best about your new boss. Focus on these positives at all times with all people, making sure your spouse and closest confidants do the same.

- *Approach:* Proactively tell your new boss you want to be part of the new team and follow up with actions that reinforce this.

- *Learning:* Present a realistic and honest game plan to help the boss learn:
  - Clarify the situation and plans, offering objective options.
  - Seek out the new boss's perspective early and often and be open to new directions.

- *Expectations:* Understand and move on your new boss's agenda immediately.
  - Know the boss's priorities.
  - Know what the boss thinks your priorities should be.
  - Decide what resources you both agree to invest in your area.

- *Implementation:* Adjust to your new boss's working style immediately. This is a hard shift, not an evolution:
  - *Control points:* Give the boss requested information, in the format desired, at the frequency wanted.
  - *Decisions:* Clarify decision making (When each of you decides. When each of you provides input.) Remember, the old rules are out. It's a new game.
  - *Communication:* Clarify the boss's preferred mode, manner, and frequency, and how disagreements are managed.
  - *Imperatives:* Readjust your team's imperative, if necessary, to match your new boss's vision.

- *Delivery:* Be on your "A" game:
  - Be present and "on"—everything done by you and your team will be part of your new boss's evaluation of you.
  - Deliver early wins that are important to your new boss and to the people the boss listens to. (In a restart, the score is reset. Your old wins and your team's old wins are history.

You Deserve It

Perhaps the most important thing to keep in mind is that you got the promotion because key people were confident that you would be successful. Those key people together probably know more about the situation than you do. Furthermore, because you're getting promoted from within, they know you. To paraphrase Virgil, if those key people think you can and you think you can, you certainly can. So, prepare in advance as much as you can. Take control of your own transition as much as you can, and accelerate team progress after the start as much as you can. If you can manage that, then you and your teams can successfully transition the batons and do great things.

Promoted from Within—Summary and Implications

You can't control the context—so prepare in advance and be ready to adjust as required:

- Understand the context (planned, unplanned, interim).
- Secure the resources and support you need.
- Go with the flow, regain control of the situation, or jump into the dirty work as appropriate.

It is hard to make a clean break—so take control of your own transition:

- Manage the announcement cascade.
- Secure your base, ensuring your old area's ongoing success and cleaning out the skeletons.

- Recognize the people who helped you along the way.
- Use the time before you start to strengthen relationships.
- Assess your predecessor's legacy and clarify what you'll keep and what you'll change.
- Manage first impressions in the new role.

There is no honeymoon—so accelerate team progress after the start:

- Evolve the stated and de facto strategies (imperatives).
- Improve operations and implement dramatic changes as needed (milestones, early wins).
- Strengthen your organization (role sort).

Downloadable TOOL 5.1
Announcement Cascade Checklist*

Stakeholders
Internal

_____

_____

External

_____

_____

Message
Platform for change

_____

_____

_____

_____

Vision

_____

_____

_____

_____

Call to action

_____

_____

_____

_____

_____

_____

(continued)

*Copyright © PrimeGenesis ® LLC. To customize this document, download Tool 5.1 from www.onboarding-tools.com. The document can then be opened, edited, and printed using Microsoft Word or other word processing applications.

Preannouncement Time Line (one-on-ones, small groups, large groups)
Prior to announcement day

_____

_____

Announcement day

_____

_____

Formal Announcement

_____

_____

Postannouncement Time Line (one-on-ones, small groups, large groups, mass)
Immediate

_____

_____

First week

_____

_____

Near term

_____

_____

Over time

_____

_____

TAKE CONTROL OF YOUR OWN START

CHAPTER 6

Embrace the *Fuzzy Front End* and Make It Work for You before You Start

Part I—**POSITION** and **SELL** yourself; **MAP** and **AVOID** land mines, Do your **DUE DILIGENCE**

The New Leader's 100-Day Action Plan

| | Fuzzy Front End | Day One | 30 | 45 | 60 | 70 | 100 |

Part II
Take control of **YOUR OWN START**

Embrace the **FUZZY FRONT END** — Take control of **DAY ONE** — Exploit key **MILESTONES** to drive team performance — Secure **ADEPT** people in the right **ROLES**

Part III
Build a high-performing **TEAM**

Decide how to **ENGAGE** the new culture — Embed a strong **BURNING IMPERATIVE** — Overinvest in **EARLY WINS** to build team confidence — Evolve **PEOPLE, PLANS, and PRACTICES**

Ongoing **COMMUNICATION** campaign

WARNING!

If you have already started your new role, this chapter may upset you. It is full of ideas for people to implement *before* they start. The best way to take charge, build your team, and get great results faster than anyone thought possible is to create time by starting earlier than anyone thought you would.

I f you have already started your new role, still read this chapter. If you have yet to tackle the things presented in this chapter, start doing them immediately. Read on to find out where you need to catch up. Further, many of the ideas in this chapter are useful throughout and well beyond Day One and your first 100 days.

Many leaders fall into the trap of thinking that leadership begins on Day One of a new job. *Like it or not, a new leader's role begins as soon as that person is an acknowledged candidate for the job.* Everything new leaders do and say and *don't* do and *don't* say will send powerful signals, starting well before they even walk in the door on Day One.

If you embrace this concept and do something about it, you increase your chances of success. This one idea can make or break a new leader's transition. New leaders who miss the opportunity to get a head start before the start often discover later that organizational and/or market momentum was working against them even before they showed up for their first full day at the office.

We refer to this bonus time between acceptance and start as the *fuzzy front end.*[1] It often comes at the worst possible time, interfering with the last days of an old job, or with time earmarked for taking a vacation, catching up with household errands, or generally unwinding a little before the big day.

The good news is that, more often than not, key elements of the fuzzy front end can be addressed in relatively short order. Even so, strive to stretch out the time between acceptance and your start date. Adding days before your official start, is one of the best ways to get more done during your first 100 days. This is the only opportunity you'll ever have to create extra time and valuable *white space*[2] before jumping into your new role.

Choose the Right Day to Be Day One

You can create time in a few ways; but the best way to stretch the fuzzy front end is by taking the action steps that we discuss later in this chapter. Besides committing to taking action, there are other ways to create fuzzy front end time:

1. Negotiate a start date to allow for a longer fuzzy front end and therefore more time for helpful activities before Day One. Start

---

[1] The early stages of a new product development process are often referred to as the *fuzzy front end.* Since we're talking about onboarding as a team development process, the term works well.

[2] Malcolm Gladwell describes the difference white space can make between success and failure in his book *Blink* (see References).

dates are often arbitrarily set by organizations eager to get a new leader started sooner. Often their roles have been open for months, and another week or two will not make a difference. Yes, in some instances they are set in stone; and if that's the case, then you'll have to rely on other ways to create time.

2. Keep the identified start date, but agree with your boss and HR to announce the official start date as some later point in time (usually a week or two later). Just because your new organization and traditional thinking defines Day One as your first official day on the job, doesn't mean that you have to accept that same definition. By having a private Day One that only your boss knows about and a later public Day One that is made in the official announcement, you are in effect stretching your fuzzy front end.

Now that you know a couple of ways to stretch the fuzzy front end, you can use it for mental and physical preparation, and for prestart meetings and phone calls to jump-start relationships and learning. Everything communicates during the fuzzy front end; and nothing says more than how you spend your time. Use it to get set up personally, gather information, listen, observe, learn, and begin leading all at the same time.

Game Changing

At first, Nathaniel did not buy the concept that he should start before his official Day One. He wanted to take some time off so that he could show up at his new job rested and relaxed. Further, he felt uncomfortable asking for meetings before he was officially on the job. Eventually he agreed to try several of our suggested actions before Day One. Here is exactly what he wrote to us in an e-mail just one week later:

> *I've already reached out to some future colleagues and some agency counterparts just to introduce myself. You're right, it is game changing. Everyone has reacted with warmth and candor, and it will make the first few weeks far more effective and enjoyable.*

Create Time, Take Action

The most successful leaders know that their 100-Day Action Plan is just a subset of their 100-day communication plan. They craft their communication plan and then act to implement that plan. In Chapters 7 and 8, we discuss the importance of how you engage the new culture and drive action with an ongoing communication campaign. Before we do that, it's helpful to have an overview of how these things fit together and into your fuzzy front end. You should use your fuzzy front end to:

- Identify key stakeholders.
- Craft your message.
- Manage your office setup.
- Manage your personal/family setup.
- Conduct fuzzy front end meetings and phone calls.
- Deploy an information-gathering and learning plan.
- Plan your first 100 days.

Identify Your Key Stakeholders

Step one is to identify your key stakeholders up, across, and down both in your organization and outside. Key stakeholders are those people who can have the most impact on your success in your new role. Many transitioning executives fail to think through this process or look in only one direction to find their key stakeholders. Others make the mistake of treating everyone as key stakeholders and end up trying to please all of them. Both of these approaches are doomed to fail.

Up stakeholders may include your boss, your indirect boss if there is a matrix organization, your boss's boss, the board of directors, your boss's assistant, or anyone else who resides further up in the organization.

Across stakeholders might include key allies, peers, partners, and even the person who wanted your job but didn't get it. The across stakeholders that executives often forget are key clients and customers (external and internal).

Down stakeholders usually include your direct reports and other critical support people who are essential to successful implementation of your team's goals. Your executive assistants should be high on this list, as they can often serve as an additional set of eyes and ears.

- *Former stakeholders:* If you're getting promoted from within, make sure to take into account your former stakeholders up, across, and down from your former position.
- *Internal board:* Your internal board is made up of the people you are going to treat differently because of their influence or impact regardless of their explicit roles in the hierarchy. You're going to treat them like board members, never surprising them in meetings and making sure they get the chance to give you informal, off-the record advice. Set the stage early and position yourself as an executive who is eager for and welcomes feedback from your internal board.

Candidates for your internal board are people who are going to have an undue influence on your boss or your ability to get things done. Think in terms of your key peers. Think in terms of people who have been with your boss for a long time, of people who seem to enjoy the mentor role, of people who are trusted advisors within the organization, or of key founders who may not have a significant role in the day-to-day operations, but still wield significant influence. Once you have identified them, develop individual relationships with them. If you are in the position to do so, play the same role for them, when appropriate.

Just figuring who all these people are can be a daunting task on its own. Fortunately, this is not something new executives have to do by themselves. Generally, there will be a human resource contact, a boss, or an internal mentor who can help identify these people.

You can often get good hints about key stakeholders from the persons who previously held your role. If they were successful, they might provide some insight. If they were not successful, they probably missed or underserved a key stakeholder, so it is important to figure out who that was and why the person was underserved. Some key stakeholders will be apparent, yet others are often hidden from view, so do not be afraid to ask when you are building your list.

While it is important to keep the key stakeholder list to a manageable size, if you are not sure initially whether someone is a key stakeholder, keep the person on the list until you can get an answer. Ignoring a key stakeholder can have a devastating impact on a new leader and might kill any chance of a successful transition. Similarly, if you are likely to confuse where stakeholders fit, have a bias to upgrade them. You are not going to get in much trouble treating an "across" like an "up" or a "down" like an "across." The opposite is not true.

Craft Your Message

We talk about communication in Chapter 8 and Appendix III. You'll need to clarify your thinking about your message before you start talking to any of your stakeholders. If you're not sure about your going-in message at this point, *stop* and think it through. You don't have to stick with it. You can evolve it as you learn. But you *must* have a going-in point of view if you're going to lead. Your message is the keystone of your communication. It should be enough to satisfy your key stakeholders' curiosity while optimizing your opportunities for learning.

Everything you do communicates, especially in the fuzzy front end and the first interactions with people after your official Day One. Again, *everything* you do and say and *don't* do and *don't* say sends powerful signals to everybody in the organization observing you and everyone in the organization who is in communication with those who observe you. Crafting and deploying your message has to do with the words you use (and don't) and the actions you take (and don't) and who you are. Be conscious of your choices. When we say *everything*, we really do mean everything communicates.

HOT TIP

Getting your message right is essential. There are things you can get by with doing "good enough." There are things you must do as well as you can. And then there's your message that has to be exactly right for you. Don't compromise on this.

Manage Your Office Setup

The perfect office that is fully stocked and completely set up to your liking does not just suddenly appear. If you are lucky, you will have a place to call your own on your first day, but most likely, it will not be tailored to fit your needs or your style. Leaders in new roles often underestimate the time, planning, and thinking required to get their office space right for what they need. Many leaders make one of two mistakes when setting up their space.

One mistake is to focus energy and attention in the first week on getting their office just right. What kind of message does that send? The other mistake is to work in a less than suitable environment for months while trying to find the time to get the office right. More often than not, that time never comes and as a result may hamper their performance. Neither option is good. The alternative solution is to get this non-mission-critical, yet important job done during the fuzzy front end.

You will need a place to work. This will involve, at a minimum, some sort of desk and chair. But, think beyond that. Do you want an office? Do you want your predecessor's office? Do you want that office to have chairs, tables, or couches? Think through how you like to work and what messages you want your workspace to communicate. Should it say, "I'm the boss? I am powerful. Enter at your own risk"? Or should it say, "Come on in, flop yourself down and tell me what's on your mind"? Big desks, with formal chairs facing them say the former. Couches and comfortable chairs around a coffee table, say the latter.

There is no right answer to any of this. But part of preparing to lead is thinking through how you want to lead and the messages you want to send. Your physical workspace says a lot about you—even before people meet you.

Other physical things about your workspace to think about include cabinets, whiteboards, flip charts, audiovisual equipment, personal computer/laptop (with e-mail access), phones, cell phones, stationery, files, and business cards. Our checklists (Tools 6.1–6.4) at the end of this chapter will make it easier for you or an assistant to get the job done for you before Day One.

Get Your Space Right for Your Best Productivity

Gerry had worked at this new company for six weeks before, in an odd turn of events, his former company decided to exercise a non-compete clause it had with Gerry that required him to resign from his new job and wait it out for 12 months. Luckily for Gerry, the second company wanted to hire him back after his noncompete expired.

We met Gerry a few weeks before he was about to reenter the second company and took him through the PrimeGenesis onboarding, or in his case, reboarding preparation. When we got to the point about personal setup, Gerry excitedly interrupted us.

"That's it!"

"That's what?"

"That's why I was so uncomfortable. I'd worked at my previous company for 23 years and never really thought about my office. Then I got here and felt uncomfortable. I always thought it was just the newness. But it's because I've always had a whiteboard in my office. I think on a whiteboard. My office here didn't have one."

The HR person sitting in promised to make sure there was a whiteboard in Gerry's office before he got there, so Gerry could "think!"

Everything Communicates ... and Not Always as Intended

Robert had joined a high-tech consulting company as the general manager of delivery and operations. Robert was tasked with professionalizing the firm's project management approach, and he smartly figured out that his task would require a significant amount of interaction with his staff of talented but young project managers. He meticulously set up his office to be inviting and relaxing, knowing that the methodologies that he would be introducing would take awhile for his staff to understand and grow accustomed to. His office was set perfectly for the task, and the environment he envisioned was set almost immediately.

Robert decided to put some personal touches in his office, and he thought it would be fun if he hung one of his detailed model planes from the ceiling of his office. Several of his project managers had expressed an interest in aviation, and Robert was certain that this would foster an even more creative atmosphere. The problem was that Robert chose to hang a World War II Nazi fighter plane. For Robert, that plane symbolized the beauty of efficient project management, but for others in the company it symbolized something quite different. Robert was genuinely shocked that some of his people had found the plane offensive. He immediately took it down and apologized, but the damage that it did to Robert was drastic and an excellent start was quickly derailed.

Everything communicates and not always what you may have intended. Be careful.

Address Technology and Security Issues Early On

As long as we are on the subject of personal setup, it is worthwhile to make sure someone is getting you access to the things that you will need. In today's technology-dominant, security-driven world, many things are essential yet we often forget their importance. Without these things, it is often impossible to get work done. Think about items such as identification cards, garage or elevator passes, computers, network access, voice mail, e-mail address, and any number of passwords. It is best if all these things are taken care of in the fuzzy front end.

Know What You Can Expect in Support

Also, it is worthwhile to identify who can help you get set up. Usually it is helpful if someone other than yourself notifies the key support staff that you will be requiring their assistance before Day One. If you have not already negotiated this up front, it is important to know whether you will have an assistant. Do you want an assistant?

What should be his or her skill set? Will you be sharing an assistant with someone else? What is his or her current workload? Will you have an assigned mentor or HR representative to help you navigate the existing culture in the early days?

One of our most enlightened clients requires new senior leaders to come into the office two to three weeks before they start so they can physically see their space and pick things like layouts and color schemes. That is an organization that truly embraces the fuzzy front end!

Manage Your Personal and Family Setup

No matter how much you try, you cannot give the new job your best efforts until you get comfortable about your family's setup. Taking the time to figure out housing, schools, transportation, and the like is not a luxury. It is a business imperative. There is no better time to get this resolved than during the fuzzy front end. If you wait, all these decisions will distract you at a time when everyone is making those first and last impressions of your performance. The first 100 days are your most important test, and you can't afford to take your eye off the ball any more than is absolutely necessary. Executives often make the mistake of assuming that their significant other will take care of all the personal and family issues, but that is usually unrealistic. The more of these issues that you can get resolved before Day One the better.

Also, whether you admit it or not, having a settled place to come home to as you transition into a new role can make a significant difference in your ability to recharge at the end of the day and on weekends. Moving and starting a new job are two of the most stressful things that can happen to you and your family, so why not make sure the two Day Ones (office and personal) do not start at the same time?

The checklists at the end of this chapter should help guide you through both your office and your personal setup. Don't underestimate the distraction that both of these tasks can cause and strive to address as much as possible in the fuzzy front end.

The main point about personal setup, both at home and in the office, is that you can get it in motion well before you actually show up. There will be enough other things to worry about in the early days of a complex transition that you do not want to be rummaging around for a computer, door key, or school for your children. Get those things settled well in advance.

Conduct Prestart Meetings and Phone Calls

Everything communicates. This includes whom you talk to, in what forum, and in what order. People will view the order in which you talk to them as a sign of their relative importance. Starting Day One, that order is indelible. The people you talk to early will feel valued. The people you talk to later will feel slighted. These early conversations can make a huge difference.

There is a physical limitation to how many people you can talk to on Day One or Week One, and so on. If the people you talk to on Day One feel valued, the people you talk to *before* Day One will feel even more valued. So be selective in the order in which you approach and talk to people. Before making your calls, think about what it might say or indicate to those folks holding a spot on your key stakeholder list. Be thoughtful, plan, and know that you are communicating even without saying a word.

The most important stakeholders are the ones who are going to be most critical to your surviving and thriving in the new role. These might include:

- Your new boss
- The most influential board members
- Critical peers—especially ones who were candidates for your new job
- Critical customers and clients
- Critical direct reports—especially ones who were candidates for your new job or who are considered to be flight risks

The impact you can make by reaching out to these critical stakeholders before you start is incalculable. Yet we are often surprised at how reluctant some executives are to set up those meetings. They often expect to encounter resistance, but rarely do. To make the process easier, here are some suggestions for starting a conversation.

"Hi Jack, I'm Jill. I'll be starting in two weeks as President. Stuart has told me that you're an absolutely critical part of the team. I didn't want to show up without getting a chance to meet you in advance."

"Bob . . . since you're such a valued customer of my new company, I can't imagine starting work without getting to know you first. I'll meet you anywhere in the world that's most convenient for you, anytime that's most convenient for you over the next month. I'd really like to have your perspective on what's going on before I start."

"Andrew . . . since you weren't on the board's search committee, we haven't met. But I'd like to spend some time with you before I start."

Leverage the Fuzzy Front End to Get Real Answers

Another reason to start communicating with key stakeholders early is that the answers you get to questions before you actually start will be different from the answers you get after you start. You are a different person before you start. You are not yet an employee or boss. You are just someone looking to make a connection and learn. The answers you get during the fuzzy front end almost always prove to be exceedingly valuable after Day One.

What You See as Possible, Just Might Define You

You should have meetings with the most important key stakeholders up, across, and down as well as phone calls with other stakeholders, if at all *possible*. This is so important that we encourage you to expand your concept of possible. For some reason, executives often think meeting with the most important stakeholder is not possible if it involves taking a flight or crossing time zones. We've had executives fly halfway around the world for hour-long meetings, and we've had them meet key stakeholders on ski lifts, cruise ships, Little League baseball fields, and the hinterlands just to get those meetings done before Day One. Possible can encompass a lot of arrangements if you are willing and creative.

There are times when fuzzy front end meetings may not be possible or a potential stakeholder may be unwilling, but it is still important to make a concerted effort to set them up. Just asking for the pre-meeting makes a favorable impact.

Prestart Conversations Have a Cascading Impact

Bill was joining a company as head of sales. Jairu, the previous, beloved, head of sales had switched over to head up client relations with the firm's largest customers. We were brought in to help Bill with his onboarding, but not until the Friday before he started. We talked to him between his son's Little League baseball games on Saturday and identified Jairu as someone Bill should reach out to if possible. He agreed, and he had what he thought was a nice, but not particularly important conversation with Jairu on Sunday.

The next day, Bill's Day One, six of his eight direct reports said that Jairu had called them the evening before. They each told Bill that Jairu had told them that he thought Bill was a "good guy" who would be an asset. Jairu could have made the transition difficult. Instead, Bill had turned him into a supporter—even before Day One.

Do Not Miss the Importance of New or Hidden Stakeholders

Stuart was joining a large bank to head up its Asian operations. He had met most of the key corporate HQ stakeholders in Zurich before he accepted the job. We were talking to him about stakeholders and job responsibilities and discovered that Stuart's new company had just bought another, smaller bank located in Germany with several product lines that would fall under Stuart. Not surprisingly, as the transaction had just been completed, Stuart had never met anyone at the acquired bank.

At our suggestion, he got on a plane and spent two days at the acquired bank getting to know its key players before he actually started his job. The people he met were amazed that he came to visit them on his own time. Even if they were concerned about other people at the HQ, they knew they were on Stuart's radar screen. Stuart learned later that his visit calmed anxieties at the acquired bank and put a temporary and eventually permanent halt to a planned mass exodus that, if it had occurred, would have directly impacted Stuart's success.

If They Can Have Early Influence, It Is Better to Meet Them Now

Ben had been offered a job as chief marketing officer of a fast-growing Internet company. On being offered, he asked if he could meet some members of the board since they were playing an active role in the company.

"What if they don't like you? We've already made you an offer."

"If they don't like me, I want to know before I accept. I'd rather have you withdraw the offer than fire me later. Plus, by letting them weigh in now, they'll have some ownership over my entry. This will help me down the road."

So Ben met them. They did not withdraw the offer and things went well. By doing this, Ben eliminated a potential risk and sent a strong message to the board that he thought their buy-in was important.

Discover Problems Early On

Elliot was about to join a small company as vice president of marketing. The search had originally been for a director of marketing. The CEO had met and hired two people he liked at that level before he met Elliot. He was so impressed with Elliot that he hired him to come in on top of the two he had just hired.

The two new directors of marketing had not started yet.

At our suggestion, Elliot had them fly over and meet him before he started.

This turned out to be a good idea because Elliot was not impressed with either one. He went back to the CEO and probed why they were hired. It came out that the CEO really had not been all that impressed with them either. But, since he hadn't met Elliot, he thought they were the best available. Elliot convinced the CEO to withdraw their offers, getting rid of two problems even before he (or they) started.

HOT TIP

Meet with critical stakeholders *before* you start: This one idea is worth a gazillion times whatever you paid for this book. Contacting key stakeholders before you start always makes a huge difference. It is a game changer.

Deploy an Information-Gathering and Learning Plan

Now that you have you have your prestart conversations set, it is important to have an approach for those conversations. Make no mistake; these conversations are most successful when you are talking as little as possible and listening as attentively as possible. They are about building relationships, gathering information, and learning. Listen and observe.

Because this is about relationships first, your first question is probably something along the lines of "tell me about yourself." You want to connect with your key stakeholders individually. You want to understand their personal wants and needs as well as their business issues. This may also be a good time to take your crafted message out for a test drive; but keep in mind this is not about you, so keep your message short and on point. Because you are here to build relationships and learn, it is not the time to tell your life story or to offer opinions on "how things should be done."

Structuring the conversations is useful. Come into these conversations with an open mind and actively listen to what your key stakeholders have to say. Doing so in a planned and thoughtful way is fundamental to maximizing the value of these conversations. We suggest breaking the conversations into learning, expectations, and implementation.

Learning

Under the learning part of your conversations, you should focus on two key areas: perceptions and strengths. Perceptions have to do with understanding each stakeholder's assessment of the situation at hand. Once you've learned a stakeholder's view of the situation, you also want to get their input in terms of the 5Cs described earlier: Customers, Collaborators, Capabilities, Competitors, and Conditions. Use each of these Cs as a guideline for your questions.

Different stakeholders will have different views of the same situation. Some will think things are going well. Some will look at upside opportunities for the future while others will tell you things are not going well and need to be turned around quickly to prevent the impending disaster. This is not a search for the one truth. This is an exercise in understanding the different stakeholders' perceptions so you can figure out how to work best with each of them.

The second part of the learning phase is the identification of strengths. It is useful to understand the different stakeholders' perceptions of what strengths exist in the organization and what strengths need to be developed for the organization to be even more successful. Feel free to ask these questions directly. The answers will provide valuable information about the organization and maybe even some insight into your key stakeholder as well.

When you receive answers to your questions, ask for examples that might reinforce the answers. These examples will provide further depth to your understanding and will also enable you to quickly switch the "we" in your stories from being about your old company (which rubs everyone the wrong way) to being about your new company (which makes people feel like you're starting to fit in).

Expectations

Early on, it is important for you to develop an understanding of how your stakeholders' view the priorities (high, low, and untouchables) of the situation. Just by learning what they consider a high or low priority will give you a valuable perspective on how to best interact with them and how their priorities may affect your ability to deliver against your own goals.

Stated priorities are not real until they have resources attached to them. So for you to determine your own and to decipher your key stakeholders' priorities, you should focus on finding out what resources (human, capital, or otherwise) are allocated to the most important and urgent priorities.

This is also an excellent time to figure out if there are any "untouchables." Untouchables are those things that may seem odd or do not have a natural fit with the larger goals of an organization or division, but might be pet projects or protected people that you should not touch. Most organizations have them; and they can be the third rail for executives who don't recognize them as untouchables. Identify them early and let them be.

The learning objectives of the conversations with your stakeholders will be different up, across, and down. Therefore, your questions will also be different for each group. With the "up," you're looking for direction. With the "across," you're looking to build mutual understanding. From the "down," you're looking to learn about their current reality and needs.

Throughout this process, your objective should be to understand. Ask questions, listen well, and remember, don't offer your opinion yet. At this point, you just don't know enough to offer an opinion, and most likely you cannot provide any reasonable direction to anybody. So don't try. Take the pressure off yourself and just ask and listen using the preceding frameworks.

Implementation of Communication

At this part of the conversation, you're looking to understand (1) how people communicate; (2) how decisions are made; and (3) what are the control points (what things are measured, tracked, reported, and how?)

You need to understand stakeholders' communication preferences in terms of mode, manner, frequency, and disagreements.

Mode

Different people have different communication mode preferences. Is it e-mail, voice mail, in-person, memos, or something else? Sending voice mails to e-mail people is as unproductive as sending e-mails to voice-mail people. Communication is useless unless and until it has been received. Many executives mistakenly assume that everyone communicates the same way they do.

      Charlie had two bosses. Neither used computers. One boss prided himself on never reading his mail, but he checked his voice mails regularly. The other boss so detested voice mail that he had his secretary type out his voice-mail messages, but he read his mail regularly. So Charlie would leave an update for the second boss via a note and then dictate the same note into the first boss's voice mail.

Manner

Manner is similar to social behavior or style. In what way or style does the stakeholder like to receive his information? Two people might say they prefer face-to-face meetings. One might want you to stop by any-time, put your feet on the desk and share early ideas. The other might want you to make an appointment with his secretary at least two weeks in advance and make sure all the key players have provided input into your PowerPoint deck before you share it with him. Each of these is a face-to-face meeting (mode), but their manner is very different.

Frequency

Shame on you if you wander in for your monthly update with your boss and she says, "Where have you been? I expect weekly updates." Shame on you if you come in for your third weekly update and your boss says, "Why are you here every week? You are a senior player. I hired you to run your operations. Come to me if there's a problem or update me monthly." Like the other elements of communication, fre-quency preferences will vary greatly; so, ask in advance.

Disagreements

Different people prefer being disagreed with in different ways, rang-ing from:

- Never disagree with me.
- Challenge me one-on-one, in private.
- Challenge me, but never let anyone outside "the family" know what you're thinking.

- Challenge me in meetings, but gently.
- Gloves off, all the time, because public challenges communicate the culture we want.

Ask about this, but don't believe the initial answers you get. Initially, start at the top of the list and wait to see how your key stakeholders (and especially your boss), respond to disagreements and challenges from others before you start disagreeing with them or challenging them.

Decisions

Decisions can be made in a variety of ways, and it's important that a new executive understand how the key stakeholders like to and expect to make decisions. Again, it comes down to asking. Chart 6.1 provides a helpful scale for understanding how decisions between you and another person can be made.

In general, you want to push things to levels 2 and 4 (either you or your key stakeholder makes decisions with input from the other). Input is helpful whether it is veto rights, consultation, or information. Shared decisions have a nasty tendency not to be made by anyone. Avoid putting yourself in that scenario.

By the way, it is not good enough to *think* you know how this process should play out, or to *assume* that your stakeholders are on the same page with you on this. Make the effort to define the major decisions clearly and *know* how they will be made. Whether you make a decision that your boss thought was his or your direct report is making a decision that you felt was yours, it usually leads to uncomfortable circumstances at best and exploding land mines at worst.

CHART 6.1   Decisions

Level	Decision Process
1	I decide on my own
2	I decide with input from you
3	You and I decide together
4	You decide with my input
5	You decide on your own

How to Manage the Process with Stakeholders	
Up	You **ask** how major decisions are made
Across	You **negotiate** how major decisions are made
Down	You **inform** how major decisions are made

That's the easy part. The trickier, and perhaps equally important part, is understanding where decision power resides in the organization. The three key sources of power are the Deciders, the Influencers, and the Implementers. It is important to consider how they interact and their impacts on the organization when you are establishing your decision-making process.

- *Deciders:* The formal decision maker as described in the organizational chart. Makes decisions. Sets rules.
- *Influencers:* People and things that influence the formal decision maker. This may include information, experts, trusted advisors, political access, staff/team support, tradition, reputation, and professional credibility.
- *Implementers:* People who control resources required to implement decisions and impact the consequences of the decisions both inside and outside the organization.

Control Points

Different organizations use different metrics and processes for controlling what is really going on. You need to know what they are so you can track what is happening. What are the key measures of success along the way? How are they tracked? How often are they tracked? How are the reported? How can you get access to them? Meetings? Reports?

There are always metrics that are important, but are not formally captured or distributed. There are always additional key indicators that are used that you won't find out about early on. Keep an eye out for those shadow control points because often they turn out to be some of the best indicators around.

In addition to control points, there is a whole set of information you should have and review before you show up for Day One. This may include key documents, financials, customers, competitors, collaborators, current capabilities, market information, business environment, macrotrends, share, distribution, pricing, merchandising, advertising, promotion, packaging, product, presence, public relations, operations, and key contacts.

Use Your Learning to Draft Your 100-Day Plan before Day One!

There is a lot to learn—the 5Cs analysis and the conversations format previously suggested are solid tools to guide you along the way; but they are not designed to be all-inclusive. Instead, think of this process as a starting point for your entry into your new role. If you follow the process to this point, you will have completed a reasonably in-depth dive into your new organization's people, plans, practices, and purpose.

It is important not so much to have learned everything before you show up, but to have a plan to learn in place. Your learning plan, like all plans, will evolve as you get more knowledgeable.

The knowledge gathered from your due diligence and your own self-study coupled with what you learn in your prestart conversations should enable you to begin to put things in context and help you figure out what you want to do on that first day, during that first week, and during those first 100 days. With this knowledge base, you can use Tool 6.1 at the end of this chapter to begin the outline of your 100-Day Plan.

Fuzzy Front End—Summary and Implications

During the fuzzy front end, you should:

- Identify key stakeholders.
- Craft your message.
- Manage your office setup.
- Manage your personal/family setup.
- Conduct prestart meetings and phone calls.
- Deploy an information-gathering and learning plan.
- Plan your first 100 days.

The prestart meetings and phone calls are a great chance to jump-start relationships by getting at learning, expectations, and implementation. You should do these tasks. The benefits are huge.

QUESTIONS YOU SHOULD ASK YOURSELF

- Do I have the time I need before I start? (And if not, can I create it?)
- Have I optimized the time I've got?
- Should I consider a different start date?
- What am I communicating during my fuzzy front end?
- Am I comfortable with my before Day One objectives?
- Is my learning plan strong enough?
- What other resources can help with my office and family setup?

100-Day Checklist*

Stakeholders

Up:

_____

_____

Across:

_____

_____

Down:

_____

_____

(Former):

_____

_____

Message

Platform for change:

_____

_____

Vision:

_____

_____

Call to action:

_____

_____

(continued)

Downloadable TOOL 6.1   (continued)

Fuzzy Front End

Personal setup:

_____

_____

Jump-start learning:

_____

_____

Meet live in advance:

_____

_____

_____

Phone in advance:

_____

_____

(Announcement cascade*):

_____

_____

Day One

_____

_____

_____

_____

_____

First Week

_____

_____

_____

_____

_____

*If promoted from within . . .

Tactical Capacity Building Blocks

Burning Imperative (by day 30):

_____

_____

Milestones (by day 45):

_____

_____

Early wins plans (by day 60):

_____

_____

Team roles (by day 70):

_____

_____

Communication steps:

_____

_____

Stakeholder List*

	Name	Position	Interaction Plan
Up	**Management and board members**		
Across	**Key peers and internal allies**		
	Customers and suppliers		
Down	**Direct reports**		
	Indirect reports		
Other			

Downloadable TOOL 6.3

Onboarding Conversation Framework*

Key questions to ask during onboarding conversations (in addition to all the questions you would normally ask).

Learning.
Give me your read on the general *situation*?

_____

_____

_____

_____

What *strengths/capabilities* are required?

_____

_____

_____

_____

Which exist now? Examples?

_____

_____

_____

_____

Expectations
What do you see as key *priorities*? Lower priorities? Current untouchables?

_____

_____

_____

_____

(continued)

---

*Copyright © PrimeGenesis ® LLC. To customize this document, download Tool 6.3 from www.onboarding-tools.com. The document can then be opened, edited, and printed using Microsoft Word or other word processing applications.

Downloadable TOOL 6.3   (continued)

What *resources* are available to invest against these priorities?

_____

_____

_____

_____

Implementation
Tell me about the *control points* (metrics and process: meetings, reports)

_____

_____

_____

_____

Tell me about some of the key *decisions* we make.
Who makes them? How?

Who	A on own	A with B's input	A & B share	B with A's input	B on own

What is the best way to *communicate* with you?
Mode? Manner? Frequency? Disagreements?

_____

_____

_____

Downloadable TOOL 6.4
Relocation Checklist*

ASAP

Get set up: Create move file, post calendar, and so on.
Choose a moving company. Get multiple bids and references.
Research schools at destination. Public? Independent?
Gather children's essential records in a secure folder to travel with you.
Choose a real estate agent at destination.
Make arrangements to sell or rent your current home.
Make travel arrangements for family and pets.
Research temporary housing options in case they become necessary.
Look hard at your possessions for things to give away or sell.
Start a log of moving expenses for employer or taxes.
Gather information about resources in destination city.

One Month before Moving Day

Complete change of address forms (for IRS, subscriptions, bills, etc.).
Obtain medical and dental records, x-rays, and prescription histories.
Set up a checking account and safe-deposit box in your new city.
Take inventory of your belongings before they are packed, ideally with pictures.
Arrange for help on moving day, especially looking after children.

Two Weeks before Moving Day

Confirm travel reservations.
Clean rugs and clothing and have them wrapped for moving.
Close bank accounts and have your funds wired to your new bank.
Check with your insurance agent to ensure you will be covered through your homeowner's or renter's policy during the move.
Give a close friend or relative your travel route and schedule.

One Week before Moving Day

Switch utility services to new address.
Prearrange for important services—such as a working phone.
Collect valuables (important documents, jewelry, etc.) from safe-deposit boxes, dry cleaners, and so on.

(continued)

Downloadable TOOL 6.4   (continued)

On Move-Out Day

Be sure valuables are secure and ready to go with you. Carry important documents, currency, and jewelry yourself, or use registered mail.
If customary, have cash on hand to tip movers.
Have water, drinks, and snacks available for movers in appropriate place.

On Move-In Day

Have camera on hand to record damages.
Have people ready to (1) check in items, (2) direct items to right place.
Have water, drinks, and snacks available for movers in appropriate place.

CHAPTER 7

Decide How to *Engage* the New Culture

ASSIMILATE, CONVERGE AND EVOLVE, OR SHOCK

Part I—**POSITION** and **SELL** yourself; **MAP** and **AVOID** land mines, Do your **DUE DILIGENCE**

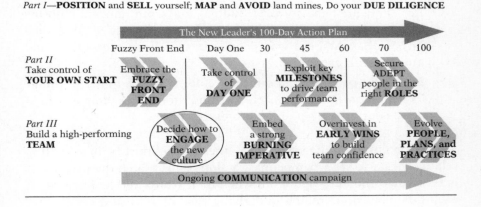

The New Leader's 100-Day Action Plan

| | Fuzzy Front End | Day One | 30 | 45 | 60 | 70 | 100 |

Part II
Take control of
YOUR OWN START

Embrace the **FUZZY FRONT END** — Take control of **DAY ONE** — Exploit key **MILESTONES** to drive team performance — Secure **ADEPT** people in the right **ROLES**

Part III
Build a high-performing
TEAM

Decide how to **ENGAGE** the new culture — Embed a strong **BURNING IMPERATIVE** — Overinvest in **EARLY WINS** to build team confidence — Evolve **PEOPLE, PLANS, and PRACTICES**

Ongoing **COMMUNICATION** campaign

You have important choices to make before Day One. One choice that you must make in advance is how best to engage with the existing culture. Cultural engagement is extremely important in a successful transition, and it is essential that executives know what their cultural engagement plan will be before walking in the door for Day One.

We have developed an ACES model, which lays out three cultural engagement choices: (1) Assimilate, (2) Converge and Evolve, and (3) Shock. After the decision to take the job in the first place, this may be the most important decision you make in your first 100 days.

You must pick the right approach if you are to have any hope of a successful transition. It is difficult, if not impossible, to recover from a wrong cultural engagement choice.

Culture can be referred to as "the way we do things here." It's the combination of what people do and say with their underlying core values. While people generally learn about culture starting with the most superficial (what people say about their culture), it's rooted in what people really are, their core assumptions and beliefs. A good shorthand we learned from one of our clients is "Be. Do. Say." It works for people and for organizations:

- *Be:* The underpinning of culture (and integrity) is what people really are, their core assumptions, beliefs, and intentions.
- *Do:* These are behavioral, attitudinal, and communication norms that can be seen, felt, or heard such as signs and symbols like physical layouts, the way people dress, talk to each other, and interact with each other.
- *Say:* What people say about their culture can be found in things like mission statements, creeds, and stories. As Edgar Schein points out,[1] these get at the professed culture.

For a culture to be sustainable, these three must be in sync. It is relatively easy to see when people's actions don't match their words. It is far more difficult to figure out when their words and actions match each other but don't match underlying assumptions and beliefs. Yet when that happens, those people's words and actions will change over time. Just as your own values, actions, and words need to line up, the same is true for an organization's.

Hot Tip

Look well beyond the professed culture: It's not that people lie about what's important to them. It's just that value statements and creeds are often aspirational. You must understand the resting, steady state norms of attitudes, behaviors, and communication that people default to "when the boss is not around."

---

[1] See Edgar Schein, *Organizational Culture and Leadership* (San Francisco: Jossey-Bass, 1985).

Whether you think much about this or not, you have deeply ingrained cultural behaviors and perspectives. They represent layers and layers of family, community, educational, and professional formation. As you assess and engage your new culture, you need to be acutely aware of your own background and behavior, and how they will come across with your new home culture. The thing about culture is that it's largely unconscious. We are often not aware of our own cultural modes until someone from a different culture points out a behavior and we think: "Hmm, it's true, I never really thought about that but I do like to do X in Y type situations."

The more aware you are of your own cultural habits, the more you can adapt and choose attitudes and behaviors that you want to embody as you move to become a successful leader. After having gone through our Five-Step Career Plan Tool (Chapter 1), you probably have thought through your values, strengths, and skills. If you've thought through how to position yourself for leadership, you will have gotten a sense of how others can perceive you (and the ways by which you can help shape that perception). If you're entering into a completely new environment, the entire process of engaging with others' perceptions of you will need to be rapid rather than drawn out because perceptions are developed and solidified almost immediately.

Identify the Core Decision-Making and Management Language

Everything that an organization does is culture. The most important dimension of this for you, as a new leader, will be how you consider and make important decisions. Every organization has a core decision-making language for processing key information and making important decisions. You will not have the leisure to study this over months. You will need to decipher it as quickly as possible.

You should get most of the way there with some logical assumptions about the business and the people you have interacted with already. Is this a technology company whose core senior management are PhDs and who have unwavering belief in the superiority of their product and product development? Is it a company that has managed to surge past competitors with high-powered marketing skills? Is it a media company with a new team of former management consultants at the helm? You can make some safe bets on how the company makes important decisions by thinking these things through.

As you proceed through the first steps of the 100-Day Action Plan, you should be testing your hypotheses, confirming, and refining. Again, asking is often the best way to go. "How do you guys go about making important decisions? What kinds of backup, presentation, defense do people expect and use?" If the answers are consistent, you know something. If the answers are highly inconsistent, you know something else, and you need to know more.

Don had had a successful career as a management consultant, venture capitalist, and most recently as chief operating officer of a mortgage company that he helped turn around. So when he was hired as COO of a high-growth company to bring in better management controls, more process, and organizational focus, he was looking forward to making an impact quickly.

On his arrival, Don quickly analyzed the various divisions of the company and gave each of them their marching orders. He rebuilt their processes, tightened up their controls, and sharpened their goals. He saw signs of early wins in some areas and, of course, resistance in others.

Donald thought he had the mandate by the chief executive officer (CEO) and board of directors to deploy in a more strategic, long-term approach, and he set about it as if he had been hired to save a failing company. The problem was that no one other than Don considered it a failing company, nor did they think he had been hired to parachute in and save it. As a result, almost everything he had done had rubbed somebody the wrong way, and Don never noticed it. He felt the culture was ready and waiting for a savior to implement drastic change while all they were looking for was a more mature and systematic approach to the way they were already doing business. Don didn't notice that he didn't have real buy-in from his key stakeholders and as a result they were determined to ignore or undermine the marching orders that Don had given. Four months after his arrival, the company posted its worst results ever and Don was history.

Don's mistake was that he had violated the core cultural code of decision making and management. He had made a fundamental miscalculation of how to engage the culture of the company, failed to build important alliances with key stakeholders and misread the CEO's and board's directive. The key cultural component that he failed to read was that the management, especially the CEO, had coalesced around a culture of consensual decision making and tactical management based entirely on slow and steady change that focused on maintaining monthly results.

Consolidate Your Understanding of the Culture Before Choosing Your Path

On the one hand, you already know more than you think you know. On the other hand, you can never really understand an organization's culture until you've been working there awhile. (Part of the problem is that by the time you know enough to really understand it, you will have become so much a part of it that you will have lost your ability to observe objectively from the outside.) Either way, pause to consolidate what you learned during your interviews, your due diligence, and your prestart conversations.

During the interviews, you observed how people interacted with you and with each other. You heard how they explained "the way things are done here" to you. You read about the organization. You learned the history, key stories, significant moments in history, respected signs and meaningful symbols, and so on.

During due diligence, you gathered information from scouts, seconds, and spies on the organization, role, and how you fit. A significant part of this was getting at "how things work" which is important data about the culture.

During your prestart conversations, you gathered information about how people perceive the situation you're going into and what they think about your priorities. Most importantly for this discussion, you gathered information about implementation. Those of you reading between the lines have already figured out that *implementation* is code for *culture*. Understanding how people really communicate, how decisions are really made, and what people really measure and track, and how things get done goes a long way in developing an understanding of the culture.

Be aware and on the lookout for subcultures. Most organizations look more like gumbo, where the ingredients coexist and complement each other without losing their individual identities, rather than like a puree, where the ingredients are blended together to create a uniform whole. The different groups within the organization have subcultures that nest within the overall culture just as the different individuals have unique personalities.

So, take what you've learned by now. Think about it and lay out what you think are the core components of the culture. Tool 7.1, Culture Assessment, can help.

Choose Your Engagement Path

Be mindful how you come in to an organization, using an ACES model to determine whether you want to Assimilate, Converge and Evolve, or Shock the organization with your entry.

ACES Framework

A: Assimilate

CE: Converge and Evolve

S: Shock

Not surprisingly, *Assimilating* is the safest way to engage the culture. If they wear white shirts, you wear a white shirt. If they leave the office at 6:15 every night, you leave the office at 6:15 every night. Whatever they do, you do. This is the least threatening approach you can take. It is appropriate when you are coming in at the helm to steer an excellent ship on an already charted steady course. When you are required to make the least amount of change and the least amount of impact, this is the way to go.

Converge and Evolve is a relatively safe middle way that will allow you to move things in the right direction over time. Here you converge with the existing culture first, and then help it evolve over time as appropriate. If they are wearing white shirts, you wear a white shirt for a while. Then, at the appropriate time, you evolve into a blue shirt on occasion. (You daredevil!)

Most of the time this is going to be the preferred approach. The trick is to know when to stop converging and start evolving. If you choose this option, know that the evolving part takes time, and as we lay out in Chapter 8, your communication plan plays a big role in your ability to evolve the culture over time. Just because the people who directly report to you are doing things the way you hoped and just because the people who report to them are doing the same thing does not mean that the people farther down the line have adopted the new culture. A detailed communication plan will help ensure that happens. Generally speaking, constantly reinforcing norms through action, rewards, and communication is the most effective way to proceed in evolving the culture.

Shock is the opposite of Assimilate. Trying to immediately jumpstart the culture to your way is the most threatening and risky move you can make. There will be active resistance and pushback. The body of the organization will try to eliminate the cause of the changes—you. Shock is something you only want to use when you must. If the ship is going down, you must. If there is nowhere else to go or no other choice, you must. Just be ready for them when they come after you.

Deciding How to Engage the New Culture— Summary and Implications

You must choose whether to assimilate into the new culture, Converge and Evolve, or Shock (ACES).

First consolidate your understanding of the beliefs, behaviors, and words that make up the culture based on what you learned:

- While interviewing
- During due diligence
- During your preboarding conversations

In the vast majority of cases, you'll want to converge and evolve, choosing carefully when to switch from converging to evolving. You should know how you plan to engage the culture, but if you choose to converge and evolve, you'll have time to decide when to stop converging and when to start evolving.

QUESTIONS YOU SHOULD ASK YOURSELF

- Do I understand the core decision-making and management language of this organization?
- Am I starting this job with a workable understanding of the big blocks of the culture?
- Have I made a clear ACES deployment choice to match the situation?
- If I choose Converge and Evolve or Shock, do I understand what parts of the culture can benefit from change?

Culture Assessment Sheet*

---

1. Say
Stated mission, vision, and so on

_____

_____

_____

Stated values, creed, and so on

_____

_____

_____

2. Do

Communication	more informal	......|......|......|......|......|......	more formal
Office layout	more collaborative	......|......|......|......|......|......	more hierarchical
Decision making	more collaborative	......|......|......|......|......|......	more hierarchical
Control points	verbal/face-to-face	......|......|......|......|......|......	written/systematic
Other notable practices			

_____

_____

_____

Downloadable TOOL 7.1

---

3. Be

Power bias	individual expertise		task focused	hierarchical	monarchical
Identity	subgroup bias	......|......|......|......|......|......			one-team bias
Conflict	avoided/destructive	......|......|......|......|......|......			welcome/ constructive
Risk appetite	protect what got	......|......|......|......|......|......			risk more/gain more
Time horizon	shorter term	......|......|......|......|......|......			longer term, multiyear
Learning	directive	......|......|......|......|......|......			collaborative/shared

Other insights

CHAPTER 8

Drive Action with an Ongoing *Communication* Campaign

Part I—**POSITION** and **SELL** yourself; **MAP** and **AVOID** land mines, Do your **DUE DILIGENCE**

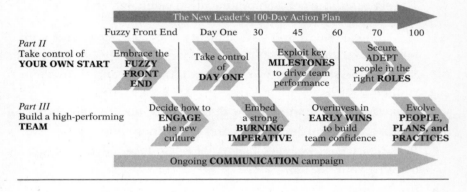

Everything communicates—everything you say and do, and everything you don't say and don't do. Furthermore, everything great leaders say and do flows directly from their own core values, beliefs, and intentions. They live their message. This is why your 100-Day Action Plan should be a subset of your overall communication plan and why you to need to think through what's really important to you, to the people you're communicating with, and what and how you want to communicate, before you say or do anything.

Since leadership is about inspiring and enabling others to do their absolute best together, in pursuit of a meaningful and rewarding shared purpose, the starting point for your communication plan should be that purpose. Your plan is about moving your target audience from its current reality toward that purpose. Think in terms of a campaign, driving a single-minded message over and over again in different ways over time.

Hot Tip

Think in terms of a *communication* campaign: Craft your core message and key communication points and drive them over and over and over throughout the organization. Effective communication is hard work. But it will be one of the most important and most enduring things you do.

The six basic steps of a communication campaign are:

1. *Plan* the campaign and key elements: message, signs and symbols, media, and touch points.
2. *Seed* the message before your start, on Day One and throughout your early days.
3. *Launch*, leveraging work on the *Burning Imperative* as appropriate.
4. *Roll out*, leveraging *milestones* and celebrating *early wins*.
5. *Reinforce* when doubters inevitably raise their heads by implementing your *role sort*.
6. *Institutionalize* by embedding key routines and processes.

Graphically the campaign looks like Figure 8.1 and Tool 8.1 can guide you in creating this.

FIGURE 8.1   Communication Campaign Flow

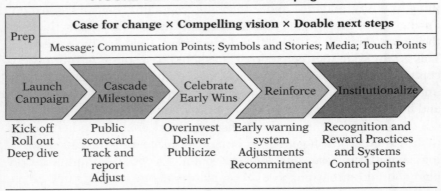

Prep	Case for change × Compelling vision × Doable next steps
	Message; Communication Points; Symbols and Stories; Media; Touch Points

Launch Campaign	Cascade Milestones	Celebrate Early Wins	Reinforce	Institutionalize
Kick off Roll out Deep dive	Public scorecard Track and report Adjust	Overinvest Deliver Publicize	Early warning system Adjustments Recommitment	Recognition and Reward Practices and Systems Control points

Plan the Campaign

To prepare, you have to get the tools in place:

- Craft an overarching message.
- Determine the key communication points.
- Choose the signs, symbols, and stories to leverage.
- Lay out your media plan.
- Map out the touch points.

Message

Great communication campaigns pivot off a central message. Think "We're going to be number one or number two or we're going to get out," used for one of Jack Welch's early drives at GE. Or "a car in every driveway" for Ford early in the past century. The point is that you need an overriding message to anchor the campaign. A good place to look for it is in the compelling vision of the future that comes out of your imperative workshop.

Writing about new Rochester, New York, schools superintendent Jean Claude Brizard, Meaghan McDermott says:

> His message for Rochester is that we must "make education personal."
>
> I read somewhere once that every child is a work of art," he said. "Our task is to help create a masterpiece out of each. We need to get teachers and principals to a place where they can track the progress of each student and create the proper enrichment and intervention for each.
>
> He said he wants to create an environment in the district where if he asks a school principal about a specific student and their dreams, aspirations, struggles and achievement, he and school leaders will be able to have a meaningful dialogue about that child's future.[1]

Leadership is personal. Your message is the key that unlocks personal connections. The greater the congruence between your own values, intentions, actions, and words, the stronger those connections will be. This is why the best messages aren't crafted; they emerge.

---

[1]Meaghan M. McDermott, "Brizard Takes City School District's Reins Today," *Rochester Democrat and Chronicle,* January 2, 2008.

This is why great leaders live their messages—not because they can—but because they must. "Here I stand, I can do no other."[2]

Often one of your communication points is also your message. So let's talk about them.

Communication Points

You can't get people to do anything different unless they believe that there is a reason for them to do that (platform for change), they can picture themselves in a better place (vision), and know what to do to be part of the way forward (call to action). Here are the three basic points you'll be driving over and over again in your communication campaign:

1. *Platform for change:* The things that will make your audience realize they need to do something different from what they have been doing.
2. *Vision:* Picture of a brighter future—that your audience can picture themselves in.
3. *Call to action:* Actions the audience can take to get there.

To illustrate these points, imagine a pack of polar bears. They are playing on an ice floe. It's melting! It's drifting out to sea! They're either going to drown or starve to death. Either scenario is not good. [Platform for change] The good news is that there's some ice nearby that's sitting on land with access to food. The bears could play there, be safe, and get food. [Vision] So, polar bears, how about swimming over to the other ice? [Call to action]

Keep in mind that everyone in the organization affected by your leadership will want to know the same thing: "How will the changes impact me?" When you are crafting your communication points, keep in mind these two principles: (1) explain how the changes will enable them to be more successful themselves, and (2) treat them decently as human beings[3] and you'll go a long way toward providing a motivating answer to that question.

---

[2] Attributed to Martin Luther at the Diet of Worms, 1521, when asked to recant his earlier writings.
[3] This thinking is derived from Amabile and Kramer's article, "Inner Work Life," *Harvard Business Review,* May 2007.

Signs and Symbols

Often, signs and symbols can speak louder than words. Some of the most compelling and telling signs and symbols (think: "Be," "Do," and "Say") include:

- How time is allocated and spent
- Chosen control point metrics and processes
- The way decisions are made
- The setting of communication norms around mode, manner, frequency, or disagreements
- If, how, and when evidence of changes in behaviors and attitudes are recognized
- If, how, and when early wins are celebrated
- If, how, and when appropriate role changes are made
- Acquisition or divestiture of companies, divisions, services, functions, and talent
- If, how, and when those who won't make the change are publicly admonished

Media Plan

Media are the methods or vehicles you choose to deliver your message. There are many ways to deliver messages including one-on-one meetings, small-group meetings, large-group meetings, phone calls, video-conferences, e-mail, voice mails, text messages, handwritten notes, and general mass communication (events, bulletin boards, intranet, chat, blogging, and pop-ups) to name a few. Not surprisingly, different media are more appropriate for different situations. Mass media is good for making a broad group of people aware of information quickly. Large groups allow for some questions. Small groups allow for more of a conversation. Face-to-face, one-on-one, is important to connect with the individuals with the most at stake personally.

Touch Points

Touch points are those areas that are touched or reached by your message. An effective communication campaign must include multiple touch points in multiple venues. You'll need to determine both the number of people you reach and the frequency with which you touch them. For the key individuals and groups that you want to touch, map out a series of media methods including face-to-face conversations, phone calls, videoconferences, notes, e-mails and more general mass communications.

Stories

Storytelling is a powerful communication tool. As Peter Guber describes in his article, "The Four Truths of the Storyteller,"[4] the most effective stories embody:

- *Truth to the teller:* sharing and conveying the deepest values with openness and candor
- *Truth to the audience:* tapping into what is important and delivering on what is emotionally fulfilling—for them (back to struggles and aspirations)
- *Truth to the mission:* driving toward a purpose that is meaningful and rewarding for the teller and for the audience
- *Truth in the moment:* fitting into the appropriate context for each audience, each time

Live the Story

Your followers won't really believe what you show or say; they will believe only what you do. This is why storytelling is necessary, but not sufficient. This is why it's so important to live your message. You must model the attitudes and behaviors you want others to follow so those others can share your understanding and your dreams, feelings, and commitment.

Seed

You generally do not want to start with a big launch that catches everyone by surprise. Instead, you'll want to seed your message with an ever-growing set of stakeholders before your launch. The seeding process gives you an excellent opportunity to test your message and delivery, observe individual reactions, and subsequently sharpen your message. Do not underestimate the power of seeding.

---

[4] Peter Guber, "The Four Truths of the Storyteller," *Harvard Business Review,* January 2008.

If you follow the steps of our prototypical 100-Day Action Plan (not that anyone does exactly), this seeding phase runs from well before your start through to your imperative workshop.

Seed Your Message—Even If You Don't Actually Say the Words

Deborah had grown up in her firm over the past two decades. When the head of the 5,000 person manufacturing organization was recruited away 7 months earlier, she had been named interim head. Now, after a thorough internal and external search, the CEO and board had just named her to the job on a permanent basis. Her plan was to spend her first two months just listening and learning. She didn't want to come out with any formal pronouncements, visions, or the like. She wanted everyone to think she was open to new ideas and new ways of doing things—especially since she was an insider.

The trouble with that approach would be its unintended consequence of making some people think she was randomly fishing without a clue. She had just been named as one of the top five officers of the firm. People looked to her for leadership and direction. When she spoke, people thought she was speaking for the CEO and board.

So, Deborah modified her intended approach. She thought things through and crafted a first, tentative, hypothetical message to focus her first two months' conversations. She still didn't come out with any formal pronouncements, visions, or the like, but her message guided her choice of which people to talk to in what order, what questions to ask, and what hints to drop. Instead of turning her mind into a blank slate, she used those two months to test and seed her message.

Deborah's company had been a star performer based on its leading edge manufacturing technologies. Deborah knew the company had to continue to invest in the technologies to stay on that leading edge. So her going-in mantra was "top-tech."

With that in mind, she started her learning tour by visiting the organization's technology innovation centers and met with its "top-tech" performers. She probed them about what had made the company successful so far and what resources they'd need to continue to be rated top tech. She visited the company's key outside partners on the technology side and asked them the same questions. She visited customers and asked them about their future needs and how the company's top tech approach could help them over time.

Then she pulled her direct reports together to craft a shared imperative, starting the day by sharing what she'd learned on her top-tech tour. Then, they cascaded that shared top tech imperative down to the next layer of management to craft a set of plans that would keep the company top in tech.

At the end of her first two months, Deborah then, and only then, sent a note to the full 5,000 people talking about all the great things they had done on the technology front to give the company a competitive advantage in manufacturing and how the top management team in manufacturing was committed to investing in them to ensure that the company stayed at the leading edge of technology-based manufacturing.

Hot Tip

Get your message vaguely right immediately. You're not going to go preach your message on Day One. You're going to evolve it over time. But you can't avoid inadvertently sending the wrong message until you know the right message for you, for them, for the mission, and for the moment.

Launch

Launches can be big, subtle, or somewhere in between, and the style of the launch should match what is comfortable for you and your team. You need to be comfortable with the method of launch, or it will show. It also needs to be in keeping with the culture of the organization, unless you are trying to shock the existing culture.

The way you launch the campaign could be one of its most powerful signs and symbols. Look at the presidential party conventions. For the most part, these days they are shows. But they know that everything communicates and they are careful about who speaks, when, and saying what against what backdrop. You should do no less.

Many of the people we work with use an imperative workshop to transition from seeding phase to launch phase. They use the imperative workshop to get their core team aligned around the Burning Imperative and then use that as the basis of their communication campaign launch.

Whatever may be your point of inflection, you will likely want to kick off the full-blown campaign with some sort of launch and follow that up with a broader rollout either through subgroup meetings or mass-communication. Your follow-up to the launch may include:

- Meetings or calls with key individuals
- Subteam workshops/meetings to gain buy-in
- Regrouping with the core team to gather input and adjust to what you learn as appropriate and practical
- "All-hands" meetings, videos, or calls
- "All-hands" e-mail confirming the direction
- Deep dive meetings with selected individuals to drive the message

Cascade Milestones

However you choose to do it, launching is a major step. But you've just begun. Now you have to make it real by proving that you are going to deliver those achievable next steps. This is where you will likely want to deploy some sort of public scorecard where everyone can see results against key milestones.

Make sure you are clear on what you are going to track. Make sure you actually do track it and report it. Make sure you're driving your key communication points at every touch point having to do with milestones—with your core team, their direct reports, and deep-dive meetings throughout the organization. Then, adjust what is going on to drive the milestones that are on track even faster and get caught up on the ones that are falling behind.

Repeat the Message

In this effort, repetition is not just good, it is essential. We'll say it again—repetition is not just good, it is essential. You will have to create different ways and times to repeat the same message over and over again. You do that with a combination of "Be," "Do," "Say." You'll get bored of your own message well before the critical mass has internalized it, but don't shy away from repeating it. Do not ever let your boredom show; make sure your energy and excitement levels are felt about the message. When you're done, do it again, fitting it into the right context for each audience each time.

Celebrate Early Wins

Somewhere along the way, you will have identified an early win for your first six months. As part of this campaign, you will have over-invested to deliver that win. When it is complete, celebrate it—and celebrate it publicly. This is all about giving the team confidence in itself. So invest your time to make the team members feel great.

Reinforce

There will be a crisis of confidence at some point. The team will question whether you're really serious about these changes and whether the changes you are making are going to stick. Be ready for the crisis and use that moment to reinforce your efforts.

The first thing you have to do is to have an early warning system in place to see the crisis developing. By this time, you should have other eyes and ears throughout the organization who can give you an "on the street" read of the situation. These are the people who feel safe telling you what's really going on. They might be administrative staff outside your direct line of reports, or they might be people far enough removed from you that they don't feel threatened telling you the truth. Whoever they are, you need to identify them and cultivate them.

The main sign of the impending crisis will be the naysayers or detractors raising their heads and their objections again or more boldly. It is likely they will go quiet during the period of initial enthusiasm after the launch of the Burning Imperative. But they will usually find it impossible to stay quiet forever. Their return to nay saying will be the first sign of the crisis and their point of view will spread if you don't cut it off.

So hit the restart button fast. Make it clear that you are committed to the changes. Regroup your core team to confirm their commitment. Take action against the blocking coalitions. This is a good time to shine the spotlight publicly on some people who are still in the way, perhaps implementing your *role sort* to move some people out. Some good steps at this point may include:

- Regrouping with your core team to gather input and adjust as appropriate.
- Holding "all-hands" meetings, videoconferences, or calls to high-light progress and reinforce the Burning Imperative.

- Sending follow-up notes confirming the commitment to the Burning Imperative.
- Making follow-up phone calls with each individual on the core team.
- Reinforcing the imperative at each key milestone with core team, their teams, et al.
- Holding meetings or one-on-ones with key people or groups at a level below your direct reports.
- Making field or plant visits.
- Implementing a structured monitoring plan.

Institutionalize the Change

Next, you'll want to put in place practices that will ensure the changes you have made so far become part of the core fabric of how you do business. Some of the ways that you can do that include:

- *Recognition and rewards:* This is a great place to start. Make sure your recognition and reward system is built or modified to recognize the behaviors and attitudes that are important to and show support for the new way of doing business. Make sure they reward the results you want and do not reward the results you do not want.
- *Mode, manner, frequency, and disagreement:* You must modify all four of these aspects of communication to fit the new business directives. This step is often overlooked, but it is very important; and once implemented, it works on its own to reinforce how and when you want things communicated.
- *Decision points:* Be sure to modify how decisions are made, pushing them as close to the customer/client as you can.
- *Control points:* Modify the control points so you are measuring the right thing with the right reporting processes.
- *ADEPT team:* Pay close attention to your ADEPT organizational process. First, **A**cquire people who will support the new direction and values and then make sure you incorporate them into your **D**evelopment and **E**ncouragement plans. Finally, **P**lan for and **T**ransition the right people throughout your team. Promotions

can be a powerful sign and symbol of what you value. (There is much more on this in Chapter 13.)

Beyond these three, there is a whole host of other supporting systems and practices that you can line up to reinforce the new way of doing business.

Where to Start and What You Need to Know

Now that you have a process and methodology for your communication plan, you're probably wondering where to start. You will want to complete the following preliminary analysis and set of questions before you begin implementing your communication plan.

Specifically Identify Your Target Audience

- Who are you communicating to? (Be specific and include everyone and all groups. Answer each one of the following questions with your entire target audience in mind.)
- What are they currently thinking and doing?
- What do they need to stop doing, keep doing, or change in the way they are doing it?
- What do they need to know to move them from their current state to the desired state

Craft the Message

- Why does the audience need to change?
- What will things look like after they change?
- What should they do next?

Plan the Campaign

- How and with whom are you going to seed it?
- When and how will you launch it?
- When and how will you cascade it?
- When and how will you celebrate wins?
- When, how, and what will you reinforce?
- How will you institutionalize it?

Implement the Campaign

- How can you make it an ongoing campaign?
- What is appropriate for mass, large-group, small-group and one-on-one communications?
- What are the plans for each?

Monitor and Adjust as Appropriate

- How will its success be measured?
- How often is success measured?
- What are the contingency plans?

It may not be essential to go into all the details and nuances at this point, but you should have as detailed answers to these questions as possible. While you will have some control over seeding your message, you should be aware that you're going to start seeding the new culture immediately—whether you want to or not. Everything that we talk about after this point is part of your communication campaign in one way or another.

Beware the Unintended Consequences of Throwaway Comments

The CEO and a member of his board of directors were walking down the hall during a break. The board member casually asked how things were going in Japan. (They were going fine.)

The CEO mentioned to the company president that the board member had asked about Japan.

Then the president told the Asia group president that the board was concerned about the company's progress in Japan.

So the group president asked the company's Japan president for a full business review so he could allay the board's fears.

The Japan president canceled everyone's vacation and travel plans in Japan for a one-week sprint to completely review and replan the business in Japan.

The board member had no idea what he was unintentionally triggering.

Make sure you do.

Remember It's Not What You Say That Counts— It's What They Hear

One general manager was working to push decision making down into his organization. Of course, he still wanted to be kept informed. At the end of a session during which one group was informing him about what they were doing, he said, "I like it. Go for it."

What he said was intended to provide positive reinforcement for decisions his subordinates were making. Some of those subordinates interpreted what he said as giving his approval. Thus his subordinates became less clear on what the general manager did and did not want approval rights on. So they started taking more and more things to him for approval—exactly the opposite of what he wanted.

The antidote to this problem is to be particularly explicit when you're not making a decision. In this case, the leader might have said something like "I applaud the decisions you're making. Thank you for keeping me informed. What do you need me to do to help?" Then the leader should figure out how they can EASE the way for their team by Encouraging them, Aligning others with them, Solving a problem for them, or Ending something that's distracting them.

We have included additional thoughts—both general and specific—about communication, culture, and change in the Appendixes. We encourage you to read them carefully.

Communication—Summary and Implications

A communication campaign's key components include:

- *Plan* the campaign and key elements: message, signs and symbols, media, and touch points.
- *Seed* the message before your start, on Day One and throughout your early days.
- *Launch*, leveraging work on the *Burning Imperative* as appropriate.
- *Roll out*, leveraging *milestones* and celebrating *early wins*.
- *Reinforce* when doubters inevitably raise their heads—by implementing your *role sort*.
- *Institutionalize* by embedding key routines and processes.

QUESTIONS YOU SHOULD ASK YOURSELF

- What is the message?
- Is the message compelling?
- Do I know how I'm going to get people to embrace that message?

Downloadable TOOL 8.1
Communication
Campaign Milestones*

	How	Who	When

Plan Ready

Message/communication points _____

Signs, symbols, and stories identified _____

Media and touch points set _____

Seed Message

Early testers _____

Early adapters _____

Other seeding _____

Launch Campaign

Kick off _____

Roll out _____

Deep dive _____

Cascade Milestones

Public scorecard _____

Track and report _____

Adjust _____

Celebrate Early Wins

Overinvest _____

Deliver _____

Publicize _____

Reinforce

Early warnings _____

Adjustments _____

Recommit _____

Institutionalize

Recognition and reward _____

Practices _____

Control points _____

*Copyright © PrimeGenesis ® LLC. To customize this document, download Tool 8.1 from www.onboarding-tools.com. The document can then be opened, edited, and printed using Microsoft Word or other word processing applications.

CHAPTER 9

Take Control of *Day One*

MAKE A POWERFUL FIRST IMPRESSION

Part I—**POSITION** and **SELL** yourself; **MAP** and **AVOID** land mines, Do your **DUE DILIGENCE**

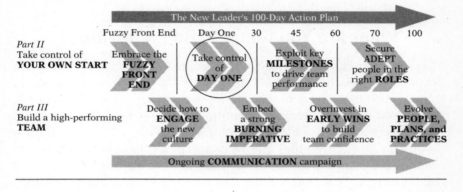

The New Leader's 100-Day Action Plan

| | Fuzzy Front End | Day One | 30 | 45 | 60 | 70 | 100 |

Part II
Take control of
YOUR OWN START

Embrace the
FUZZY FRONT END

Take control of **DAY ONE**

Exploit key **MILESTONES** to drive team performance

Secure **ADEPT** people in the right **ROLES**

Part III
Build a high-performing
TEAM

Decide how to **ENGAGE** the new culture

Embed a strong **BURNING IMPERATIVE**

Overinvest in **EARLY WINS** to build team confidence

Evolve **PEOPLE, PLANS, and PRACTICES**

Ongoing **COMMUNICATION** campaign

Our brains remember information "presented first and last, and have an inclination to forget the middle items."[1] People will remember vividly their first impressions of and their last interaction with you. While you can update their last interaction constantly, you are going to be stuck with those first impressions. So, be careful when choosing them. Be careful about the messages you send with your words, with your actions, with the order of your actions, with the signs and symbols you deploy. This is why Day One is the pivot point for onboarding. Many people that are important to your new role will form their first, indelible impression of you on this day.

---

[1]Elizabeth Hilton, "Differences in Visual and Auditory Short-Term Memory," *Indiana University South Bend Journal*, 2001, Volume 4.

There is no one right way to do this, but there are many wrong ways to do this. It is all about the first impression *received*. Different people will have different impressions of the same thing depending on their perspective and filters. The problem is that prior to your first interactions with them, you can't understand their perspective and filters. So not only is there no one right answer, it will be difficult to figure out the best answer for your particular situation. This is another reason it is so valuable to get a jump-start on relationships and learning during the fuzzy front end. Not only does that let you manage your initial impressions on those people outside the noise of Day One, it will help you make better choices about your early days.

What Are You Going to Do on Day One?

That question, more than any other, stumps our clients. Most leaders fail to think about and plan Day One as thoroughly as it deserves. In fact, even those leaders who do a phenomenal job throughout the fuzzy front end find themselves stumbling at Day One. For some reason, leaders are often lulled into complacency when deciding what to do on Day One. Often they passively accept a schedule that someone else has planned out for them. Or they plan to do what seems to be the traditional Day One activities of meeting those people "around" their office or filling out the required forms, unpacking, and setting up their office.

Not you. What you say and do on Day One is going to inspire others. Not with cheesy motivational tactics, but through meaningful words and actions that create excitement about the things to come. Do not underestimate Day One's importance. Plan it with great care and make sure it communicates your message, exactly as you want it, to the people you most want to reach.

No two leaders' first days will ever be the same because the combination of variables in every situation begs for different Day One plans. However, when planning your Day One, there are some general guidelines and principles to consider:

- *It is personal.* As a leader, you impact peoples' lives. Those people will try very hard to figure out you and your potential impact as soon as they can. They may even rush to judgment. Keep that in mind at all times.

- *Order counts.* Be circumspect about the order in which you meet with people and the timing of when you do what throughout Day One and your early days.

- *Messages matter.* Have a message. Know what you are going to say and not say. Have a bias toward listening. Know that strong opinions, long-winded introductions, and efforts to prove yourself immediately are rarely, if ever, good Day One tactics. People will be looking to form opinions early. Keep that in mind while deciding when to listen, when to share, what to ask, who to ask, and how you answer. When speaking keep it brief, on point, and meaningful.

- *Location counts.* Think about where you will show up for work on Day One. Do not just show up at your designated office by default.

- *Signs and symbols count.* Be aware of all the ways in which you communicate, well beyond just words.

- *Timing counts.* Day One does not have to match the first day you get paid. Decide which day you want to communicate as Day One to facilitate other choices about order and location.

Tool 9.1 provides a convenient checklist for thinking about these things.

Make Careful Choices about Your Day One Plan

Using the preceding guidelines and your knowledge gained during your fuzzy front end, you should be well positioned to start planning how your Day One should take shape. Look for indications of what actions might be especially effective and powerful and work those items into your agenda, if possible.

Many of our clients have found value in holding early meetings with as many of the people in their reporting line as they can muster—in person, by videoconference, by teleconference, or the like. These early meetings give everyone a chance to lay their eyes on the new leader. It does not really matter what you say in this meeting because no one will remember much beyond "Hello" unless you make a mistake. If they do remember, they'll probably remember the things you wish you'd never said. So, we advise new leaders to say "Hello. Nice to be here." and not much else at this point.

Another tool our clients have found valuable is the New Manager's Assimilation Session. We have included a template for this at the end of this chapter (Tool 9.2). It is easy to deploy and is an effective tool that allows all the questions that everyone really wants to ask to be brought forward in a forum where a critical mass can hear what you have to say all at the same time. This prevents person A from filtering the message to person B who filters it again and so on. There will always be rumors. But this process, originally created by Lynn Ulrich of the Jarvis institute and deployed in great depth at GE, goes a long way toward squelching most of the rumors, innuendos, and misinformation.

Don't Reinvent the Wheel—Start with Our Prototypical Agenda

While no two executives' Day Ones are ever the same, it's often easier to start with a model. You can use the following sample agenda as a guideline for crafting your own Day One:

- Early morning meeting with your boss to reconfirm and update
- Breakfast meeting with broad group to say hello (and not much more)
- One-on-one meetings as appropriate
- New Manager's Assimilation (Tool 9.2) over lunch with direct reports and their direct reports
- Afternoon activity/meetings/walkabout to reinforce key message
- End-of-day cocktails/coffee/social for more informal greetings
- Courtesy notes, voice mails for thank-yous or follow-up, where needed and appropriate

We have used many variations of this agenda and ones that don't look anything like it. This format is a good fit for the straightforward, vanilla, most-likely scenarios. Use it as a guideline, and if you alter it, know why you are deleting something and why you are adding something else.

Perhaps the best way to get across the power of a well-planned Day One is through examples such as the following samples of some of our clients' Day One experiences.

Leverage Your Agenda as a Symbol of What's Important

Edgar was joining a company as CEO. He told us the most important thing he had to do was to change the mindset of the organization to become more customer focused.

"What are you doing Day One?"

"I've got this planned. I'm showing up, introducing myself to the team, and launching five committees to tackle the five most important priorities."

"What happened to being more customer focused?"

"What do you mean?"

"How does your planned Day One demonstrate that your main goal is to become more customer focused?"

"I guess it doesn't."

"What does it say to your customers?"

"Well, nothing, they won't know about it."

"Exactly."

Edgar changed his plans. He did introduce himself to the team, but then explained, "I'm leaving now. Because, before I'm prepared to talk to any of you about anything, I want to get out and spend some time with our customers."

Edgar then proceeded to talk to customers . . . for the next 10 days. On the third day, the chairman called him to express his concern. "What are you doing traipsing around the country? I hired you to run the business."

"I can't do that until I've learned a little about our customers."

By the end of the first week, customers started calling the chairman to tell him how impressed they were with the new CEO. "He listens. We're excited about him."

Finally, Edgar came back into the company with a comprehensive understanding of what the customers wanted and knowledge of where his company was falling short. He shared that knowledge with his new team. He met with his direct reports one-on-one to get their perspective on the customers and then used all that information to craft a Burning Imperative around a customer centric vision.

He took the message forward by calling the top 50 managers together to tell them how the new company imperative was crafted with their input as well as the customers. He explained how the imperative drove the priorities. He said, "Based on our jointly developed imperative, I'm happy to announce the formation of five committees to work on our top five priorities."

Although the top five priorities were essentially the same as he'd originally planned, they contained powerful nuances that better fit the customers' needs, and his initiative had significantly more credibility because he involved the customers and his staff. His early actions sent a strong communication about the customer's role in the company going forward.

Choose Location, Signs, and Symbols with Care—People Will Notice

Thomas lived in Singapore and joined a large bank as head of their Asia group. He was going to work out of the Singapore office for a few months and then move to their Asia headquarters in Tokyo.

"What are you going to do on Day One?"

"I thought I'd go into the office, do paperwork, and start meeting people."

"Which office?"

"Singapore."

"Why?"

"Because I'm here. Why not?"

"Because you're the head of Asia and the Asian headquarters is in Tokyo. If you start in Singapore, you'll be perceived as the head of the Singapore branch until you show up in Tokyo in January."

So, instead of starting in Singapore and doing paperwork, Thomas and his wife flew up to Tokyo and took his direct reports and their spouses out to dinner the night before he started. Then, at 9:00 AM Tokyo time, Thomas arranged a videoconference and introduced himself to his 256 regional employees while standing in the middle of the Tokyo trading floor. Then he met with direct reports during the day. Finally, to cap off his first day, he took the bank's largest customer in Japan out for dinner.

Do you see how those actions represent a big difference in terms of location, signs, and symbols? Everything communicates. Showing up to do paperwork in Singapore sends a very different message from showing up and taking charge at the headquarters.

Understand the Culture

Buell was moving into a company as head of marketing. We were on the phone with him and their director of human resources. Fresh from Thomas's success in Asia, we suggested a similar dinner with spouses for Buell's team. When the director of human resources explained that their company never did anything with spouses, Buell modified it to be dinner without spouses. Deploy different tools for different situations.

Don't Necessarily Go Where Your Boss Is

Gerry was starting work in London, but most of his direct reports were in a newly acquired company in Birmingham. During his fuzzy front end, Gerry learned that the Birmingham folks were concerned that they would be required to move to London as a result of the merger. That wasn't the case, but Gerry realized that it could become a crippling fear. So he chose to spend Day One in Birmingham to ease people's fears and to address the rumors up front. He used the New Manager's Assimilation tool to extract the common fears of the Birmingham group and went in with a strong and credible message that their jobs and their location were safe. To further underscore the message, he set up an office that was complete and functional and hired a secretary at the Birmingham office before his Day One meetings.

On the other hand, Khalil was coming in to run three divisions of a different company. The largest was in Odessa near where he lived. The second largest was in Omaha, and the smallest was in Lawrence. His boss's office was in Lawrence. Khalil chose to spend Day One in Lawrence, attending his boss's staff meeting in the morning and then spending the afternoon with the division that reported to him. For Khalil, it was important to signal to his boss that, even though he was living in Odessa, he was going to be available to be part of his boss's team.

Leverage Your Message on Day One

Karen was coming into a bank to merge three divisions into one.

"How are you going to get to know the people at each division?"

"I'm in luck. Each division manager has an offsite meeting already planned for my first two weeks. I'm going to use those as a chance to meet the key players and get to know them."

"Will that be the first time you meet them?"

"Sure, why not?"

"Because it doesn't match with your main objective or your message."

The problem was that Karen's individual divisional meetings perpetuated the culture of three different divisions as opposed to one combined group. Each of the divisions were in close proximity to each other; so to set a new course, Karen rented a theater for Day One and invited the entire staff of each division. Then she introduced herself to the entire staff of the new division at the same time. She followed this with a social event designed to get the three divisions mingling.

She eventually went to the old division's off sites, but only after setting the stage for the new, combined division.

Be Present

Kim was coming into a new company as CEO. The old CEO and founder was going to stay on as chief innovation officer.

"Tell me about Day One."

"Oh, I'm all set. I am going to get in early to get my office set up. Then I am meeting with the old CEO from nine to eleven. Then meeting with the CFO from eleven to twelve. After lunch I'm going to take care of some logistics and work on my messaging for my first official communication with the company."

"Are you a hermit?"

"What a silly question. Of course not."

"Well, if I work for you and if I haven't seen you by noon of your first day I'm pretty convinced you're either a hermit, or shy, or are not too concerned about 'us' since all you've done is lock yourself in your office."

Instead, Kim called a meeting of the company's top 100 managers at 8:30. She introduced herself, told everyone how glad she was to be there. She then had meetings with the old CEO and CFO. But, at this point, it was okay because she'd made an initial connection with her team.

Be Mindful of the Unintended Consequences

Arthur was moving from California to Montana to head up human resources at a large corporation. When asked what he was doing Day One he suggested he was going to spend it in a human resources orientation. We get this answer often from leaders, and we generally strongly suggest that they do otherwise. We love enlightened human resource leaders, and we work with many of them, but the fact remains that most company human resource orientations are not something a senior executive should be allocating his time to on Day One. Almost always, that is best done during the fuzzy front end. But, since Arthur was the head of human resources, we did feel there was some value in him experiencing the human resource orientation. But, we still suggested he redefine his approach to Day One.

In the end, Arthur pushed back his official Day One so that he could go up to Montana a week early. He used that created time to meet with most of his key stakeholders. On his official Day One, he sat through every minute of the HR orientation, brooking no interruptions. It sent a message to his team that human resources was indeed important; and it allowed him to have an informed opinion of the orientation process and how it needed to change.

At the end his Day One, Arthur bumped into the CEO who asked him how things were going so far. So Arthur told him about the pre-meetings with peers and teams as well as his positive impressions of the HR orientation. The CEO could not figure out how Arthur had gotten all that done in just one day.

Dress to Fit In

Jeb got invited to a meeting at a golf club on a Saturday morning. He was told the dress was business casual. But, since he was in Japan, he suspected that might mean something a little different. So he wore grey flannels, a formal shirt and blazer. As it turned out, he was the only one not in a suit and tie.

Conversely, Dave joined a company where people dressed casually—jeans, shorts, flip-flops, T-shirts—even to the most formal meetings. He noticed that during his fuzzy front end, but still decided to show up in a suit on Day One because he thought it signified leadership. After two months, he was still wearing a suit to work. No tie, but the suit trousers and jacket. People thought he was clinging to the armor of his old ways and that he was turned off or disapproving of the new culture. His direct reports even referred to him as "The Suit." He should have lost the suit (or just shipped it to Japan) before Day One.

Think carefully about Day One. Think about how you want to learn and communicate. Do you want to start by meeting your team in the office or off-site? Should your meetings be structured as one-on-ones or as a group? Do you want to start with a full-company meeting? Do you want to start with casual meetings? Do you want to start by telling them about you or learning about them? Do you want to start with the team or with customers? From the preceding examples, you can deduce that there is no one right answer. But just by asking yourself the questions and answering thoughtfully, you will be miles ahead of the game.

What Not to Do on Day One

You probably would not believe some of the stories that we could tell you about silly things leaders have done on Day One. Some actions have boggled our minds, but we'll leave the really bizarre stories aside and just list a few common mistakes on Day One. Please:

- Don't leave to look for an apartment or home.
- Don't show up late.
- Don't have lunch meetings with former colleagues.
- Don't consume alcohol at lunch.
- Don't tell anything but the mildest joke.
- Don't spend excessive time on the phone setting up logistics for your move.
- Don't dress inappropriately.
- Don't decorate your office.
- Don't say anything (good or bad) about your former company.
- Don't say anything negative about anybody in your new company.
- Don't use a PowerPoint presentation to introduce yourself.
- Don't schedule a doctor's appointment.

- Don't tell too much information about your personal life.
- Don't panic if things go awry.
- Don't mention that you read our book if you do any of the things that are on our don't do list.

HOT TIP

Manage Day One: Even though everything communicates, some communication is more important than others. How you spend Day One leaves an indelible impression. Control the agenda, even if you have to redefine which day is Day One.

Day One—Summary and Implications

At the start of a new role, everything is magnified. Thus it is critical to be particularly careful about everything you do and say and don't do and don't say—and what order you do or say them in.

QUESTIONS YOU SHOULD ASK YOURSELF

- What am I doing on Day one? What does it communicate?
- Am I being careful about all the ways I am communicating on Day One?
- Am I making the impression I want to make on the people I choose to make it on?
- What is my message and does my Day One agenda support it?

Downloadable TOOL 9.1
Day One Checklist*

Official Day One:

_____

_____

Effective Day One in role:

_____

_____

Your message:

_____

_____

Plan entry:

_____

_____

_____

_____

_____

Initial large-group meeting(s):

_____

_____

_____

_____

Downloadable TOOL 9.1

Initial small-group meeting(s):

_____

_____

_____

_____

New manager assimilation?

_____

_____

Other internal stakeholder meetings:

_____

_____

_____

_____

_____

External stakeholder meetings:

_____

_____

_____

_____

External stakeholder phone calls:

_____

_____

_____

Downloadable TOOL 9.2

New Manager's Assimilation Session*

The Ulrich/GE new manager assimilation process gets questions on the table and resolved immediately that would fester without it. This is a very useful session to conduct in the first days or weeks of a new leadership role.

Step 1: Provide a Brief Introduction and an Overview of the Objectives of the Session and Review the Process with all Involved (Team and New Manager).

Step 2: Team Members, without the New Leader Present Generate Questions About:

 (i) The new leader (you—professional, personal, including hopes, dreams, rumors, preconceptions, anything).

 (ii) The new leader as a team manager (what the leader knows about the team, priorities, work style, norms, communication, rumors).

(iii) The new manager as a member of the broader organization (what the leader knows about the organization, how he or she fits, priorities, assumptions, expectations, rumors).

Plus the team should answer the following questions that they'll present to the new leader:

 (i) What does the new manager need to know to be successful in this new role?
  What are the top three issues?
  What are the secrets to being effective?
  Are there any ideas for the new leader?

 (ii) What significant issues need to be addressed immediately?
  Are there any quick fixes that are needed now?
  Are there any difficult areas of the business that the new leader should know about?

(iii) Other questions and ideas?
  What is the one question that you are afraid to ask?
  What additional messages do you have?

Step 3: New Manager Rejoins Teams to Answer Questions, Listen, and Learn.

---

*Copyright © PrimeGenesis ® LLC. To customize this document, download Tool 9.2 from www.onboarding-tools.com. The document can then be opened, edited, and printed using Microsoft Word or other word processing applications.

YOUR 100-DAY ACTION PLAN

CHAPTER 10

Embed a Strong *Burning Imperative* by Day 30

*Part I—***POSITION** and **SELL** yourself; **MAP** and **AVOID** land mines, Do your **DUE DILIGENCE**

The New Leader's 100-Day Action Plan

| | Fuzzy Front End | Day One | 30 | 45 | 60 | 70 | 100 |

Part II
Take control of
YOUR OWN START

Embrace the **FUZZY FRONT END** · Take control of **DAY ONE** · Exploit key **MILESTONES** to drive team performance · Secure **ADEPT** people in the right **ROLES**

Part III
Build a high-performing **TEAM**

Decide how to **ENGAGE** the new culture · Embed a strong **BURNING IMPERATIVE** · Overinvest in **EARLY WINS** to build team confidence · Evolve **PEOPLE, PLANS, and PRACTICES**

Ongoing **COMMUNICATION** campaign

You can control your schedule during the fuzzy front end—mostly because no one expects you to do anything. You can probably control your schedule on Day One or, at least, have a big influence on it—mostly because no expects you to have thought it through as much as you have. Your control will be far less over the rest of your first 100 days—because all sorts of people will be putting all sorts of demands on your time. Carving out team-building time is going to be tough. But building a high-performing team is essential. So make the time.

Creating the Burning Imperative

On top of everything else you have to do, and all the other demands on your schedule, make the time to implement the building blocks of tactical capacity. The starting point, and indeed the foundation, is the Burning Imperative with its components of headline, mission, vision, objectives, goals, strategies, and values. Experienced, successful leaders inevitably say that getting people aligned around a vision and values is the most important thing they have to do.

The *Burning Imperative* is a clear, sharply defined, intensely shared, and purposefully urgent understanding from each of the team members of what they are "supposed to do, *now*" and how this imperative works with the larger aspirations of the team and the organization.

The Burning Imperative must have a shorthand summary or headline—most likely containing a strong, action-oriented verb. This is a brief statement, or tagline, that reminds each team member of the entire range of work—from mission through strategy and the statements behind each step—and specifically of their commitments and responsibilities in relation to that work. For example, *"Embed a strong Burning Imperative by day 30."*

To be clear, a Burning Imperative is different from a shared purpose. The difference between the two is really in the element of timing. The shared purpose drives the long-term while your Burning Imperative drives the next phase of activity on the way to the long-term. Remember the Apollo 13 example of *"get these men home alive."* Clear. Sharply defined. Intensely shared. Purposefully urgent. It trumps all petty concerns. It didn't replace the overall shared purpose of exploring the universe to increase man's knowledge. The Burning Imperative moves the team forward on the way to that longer-term shared purpose. That's what you're aiming for.

Don't Hesitate to Burn Rubber on the Way to a Burning Imperative

The Burning Imperative drives everything everyone does every day. More than any single other factor, this is what distinguishes highly successful teams from teams that flounder and fail. More than any single other factor, this is the key to surviving and thriving in a complex transition. This is the heart of tactical capacity. Teams with a clear Burning Imperative can be more flexible in their actions and reactions because each individual team member can be confident that their team members are heading in the same direction.

Not everyone agrees on how fast you should move to get this in place. The argument for stretching out this process is that the risks of picking the wrong imperative are greater than the risks of moving too slowly. There have certainly been cases where this has been true. If things are going well, there's less urgency to change things.

However, failing to track and build momentum early can create problems of its own. If some negative external factor intervenes before you have started to track and move (e.g., you lose a key customer or a vital team member leaves), you may fall into a debacle. We all have seen that the pace of change is accelerating as information flows more and more freely. In that environment, even if things are going well, competitors are going to rapidly converge on your position.

Thus you need to move quickly. Today, it is better to get moving and adapt as appropriate. Yet, how fast should you move on this? Fast. Give it good thought, but get this in place by the end of your first 30 days.

Harold was 100 days into his new role as vice president of marketing for a $1 billion manufacturing company when his boss asked him to pick up business development as well. (Harold had handled the initial steps of his complex transition well indeed.) So Harold hit a restart button with the new team, pulling them together for one of our imperative workshops.

They agreed on their Burning Imperative: *"create opportunities beyond the current horizon"* and the mission statement, vision, objectives, goals, strategies, and plans that led into and flowed out of that. Then they got input from some key divisional stakeholders. They rolled it up to the division presidents and finally to the CEO, who agreed with the plan.

What is extraordinary is not so much what they did, but how fast they got it done. From the moment this team first came together until the time the CEO approved the plans was 30 *hours*. To achieve this, they followed the outline as detailed in the Imperative Workshop (Tool 10.1) at the end of this chapter. On its completion, one member of the team said, "I've been here six years. It's the first time I've known what I was supposed to do."

HOT TIP

The Burning Imperative: This is the centerpiece of tactical capacity. When people talk about getting everyone on the same page, this is that page. Use whatever methodology you would like to get it in place. But get it in place and get buy-in early. In a hot landing with an acute need for the team to act, it's not so much that there are diminishing returns to doing this after day 30. There's a cliff. After day 30, the sense of urgency dissipates almost immediately and things start slipping precariously. So you really need to do whatever it takes to get this done by day 30. This is a big deal. We feel strongly about this.

The components of the Burning Imperative are headline, mission, vision, objectives, goals, strategies, and values. These drive the team's actual plans and actions. If you are unclear about the difference between all these things and how they work together, stop. Go to Appendix IV for a more detailed explanation. It will be well worth your time to get familiar with these basic building blocks of leadership.

Burning Imperative

- *Headline:* All-encapsulating phrase or tagline
- *Mission:* Why are we here, why do we exist, what business are we in?
- *Vision:* Future picture—what we want to become; where we are going
- *Objectives:* Broadly defined, *qualitative* performance requirements
- *Goals:* The *quantitative* measures of the objectives that define success
- *Strategies:* Broad choices around *how* the team will achieve its objectives
- *Values:* Beliefs and moral principles that guide attitudes, decisions, and actions

People often confuse the difference between a mission and a vision. Sometimes people just combine the two. But they are different. A mission guides what people do *every day*. It informs what roles need to exist in the organization. A vision is the picture of *future success*. It helps define areas where the organization needs to be best in class and helps keep everyone aware of the essence of the company.

Similarly, people confuse objectives and goals. Objectives connect qualitatively with the Vision. Goals *must* be quantitative. They must be SMART—**S**pecific, **M**easurable, **A**chievable, **R**ealistic, and **T**ime bound. Teams will often resort to a shorthand referring to a goal such as 10, 10, and 10! (10 new high-level prospect meetings, 10 new contracts, and 10 final deliverables accomplished). But as the leader, you need to make sure you keep connecting this with the objective—(Ensure a stable pipeline of new business and deliver reliably against it!).

The example of Harold and his team is real. What emerged from this Burning Imperative was a much clearer understanding by all three main parties—business development, senior management, delivery team—that each group had to ensure all parts of the pipeline, with delivery helping out with new prospect meetings, and business development helping lock down actual delivery (managing expectations and time table), and senior management paying close attention to the balance and rhythm of resources and pitching in directly as needed.

The company had experienced serious problems from an unbalanced pipeline in the past but had been unable to frame the problem and the solution. Everybody walked away from the workshop with an absolutely clear and precise sense of the role they were to play in driving the mission, vision, objectives, goals, strategies, and values of the company. "10, 10, and 10!" was the rallying cry.

The interesting thing that came out in the workshop was that each group had to formally acknowledge responsibility and commitment to the other teams' specific objectives. Once the "10, 10, and 10!" war cry started circulating, people started adding onto and playing with it. At one point, the frontline and back-end groups had estimated that roughly 10 percent of their time should be spent with the client helping the other side deliver their objectives.

So people would start meetings or conversations with "10 percent?" And the answer was, with a smile, "10 percent!" The senior management took to responding, "90 percent!" and so on. The CEO realized the team had spontaneously produced a terrific communication platform and brought up 10, 10, and 10 and 10 percent as well as all sorts of other 10-based measures and symbols in his e-mails and presentations.

Like the "10, 10, and 10!!" war cry in this example, the best Burning Imperative headlines work in part because they can get translated into something different by each team and players within the teams.

One organization was driving "winning combinations." Its various subteams interpreted that as winning combinations between the firm and customers, winning combinations between two merging firms, winning combinations between functional groups within the geography, winning combinations between local and global stakeholders.

Sometimes the mission works as a headline. Sometimes the vision or priorities work. It doesn't matter. All that matters is getting everyone on the same page.

Make It Happen

How do you build the individual elements—mission, vision, values, and so on—and roll them up into a Burning Imperative? You and your core team need to invest time and work into conceiving, shaping, articulating, and communicating each element and then helping translate these into a unified Burning Imperative that works as shorthand for the entire plan and that focuses individuals on their particular roles and responsibilities. It may seem daunting, but once it gets going and the team connects with the project, it develops a momentum and urgency of its own. The light clicking on for the team is one of the most exciting and memorable feelings you and they will ever have.

There are different ways to do this. We have used workshops with great success. The workshop tool in this chapter (Tool 10.1) is designed to help you and your team reach consensus on your mission, vision, objectives, strategies—and often values—in a single, day-long session.

The operative word is *consensus*. You probably already have a mission, vision, objectives, strategies, and values in your head. They may even be down on paper. Your team may have told you they agree. But, do they know them off the top of their head? Do they (did they ever) really believe them? Do the mission, vision, objectives, strategies, and values really drive their actions? Do they really see what they're doing as imperative or just something nice to do to pass the time of day?

Bryan Smith lays out different ways of rolling out ideas: telling, selling, testing, consulting, and co-creating.[1] We like the word and the concept of *co-creating*. The rewards of "creating together" are so immense and so memorable that the process alone is the strongest antidote to forgetfulness and indifference: "Oh yeah, the mission, what was that again? Some buzz words Susan threw down at us"; that is the destiny of many so-called imperatives. The premise behind the one-day workshop is to co-create the imperative with your core team so it is truly shared by all. Then, roll that out by letting others in the organization consult with your core team. You should be open to wording changes and some new ideas during the rollout but preserve the meaning of the Burning Imperative that you and your team co-created.

Do not make the mistake of attempting to let an entire organization co-create its imperative. There is a limit to the size of effectively creative teams, just as there is probably a limit to an effective college seminar size. Everybody needs to participate and when it would take two hours just to have everybody speak for two minutes (e.g., to introduce themselves) you know you're in trouble. If the co-creating team is too large, you're likely to end up with something that is acceptable to most and inspirational to none. By co-creating with just your core team, you can lead the team toward more inspirational ideas. Think seven people ± two as a target.

Done right, an imperative workshop is an intensive session with a lot of personal sharing and dialogue. Expect to learn a lot about your team. Expect them to learn a lot about you. It is possible that you'll end up with an imperative very close to what you came in with. It is more likely you won't. Even if you do, there's power for all in the learning. As T. S. Eliot says in "Little Gidding":

> We shall not cease from exploration.
> And the end of all our exploring
> Will be to arrive where we started
> And know the place for the first time.[2]

---

[1]Bryan Smith, *The Fifth Discipline Field Book* (Nicholas Brealey Publishing, 1994).
[2]T. S. Eliot, "Little Gidding," in *Four Quartets* (New York: Harcourt Brace Jovanovich, 1943).

Workshop Attendance and Timing

In the real world, you'll be taking over an existing team with existing priorities and existing schedules. It is unlikely that your team members will have planned to take out a day from their current work to sit around, hold hands, and sing folk songs. First point, this is real work and the imperative workshop tool is focused on real business issues. It ends up being a strong team-building exercise, but as a by-product of the work. Even so, there will be some team members who are reluctant to adjust their existing schedules to accommodate this workshop, particularly if you push to hold it sometime in your first 30 days.

Stick with the plan. Find the date in your first 30 days that works best for most people and then give the others the option to change their schedules or not. This approach has two advantages:

1. It keeps things moving forward in line with the 80 percent rule. Not everything is going to be perfect. Not everyone can be at every meeting. You and your team will move forward as best you can, helping others catch up and adjusting along the way.

2. It gives you early data about different team members' attitudes and commitment. Everything communicates; and everything communicates both ways. By inviting people to an imperative workshop, you are sending a powerful message. Their turning it down because they have something more important to do returns a different message. How you handle overt resistance will be an important early test of your ACES model.

Follow Through Consistently

Follow through and then, follow through again. Pulling people together, investing the time in this, and then not living by it, is worse than not doing it at all. A strong Burning Imperative is a covenant of honor. Once you put it in place, you must live it if you expect people to follow your lead. You must follow through on your commitments. You must support people flexing standard procedures in pursuit of the Burning Imperative.

Gerry was a volunteer with his local life squad/ambulance service. One day he heard an accident while raking leaves in his front lawn. He ran down to the end of the street and started treating the victims, enrolling bystanders to summon the police, life squad, and help in other ways. Two of the victims walked away and two had to be taken to the hospital.

After the run to the hospital, Gerry was at the station helping to clean out the ambulance for the next call when the life squad captain walked in.

"Gerry, I noticed you were on the scene of this accident without your red life squad coat on."

Gerry explained why he had gone straight to the scene without putting his coat on, going to the station, and riding with the ambulance even though he had been on call.

"But wearing your coat is important so people can identify you as a life squad member."

"Good point. I'll be careful the next time. . . . Wait a minute. How did you notice I wasn't wearing my coat?"

"I drove by."

"Are you telling me you drove by the scene of a two-car accident, saw that I was the only life squad member there and you chose to come by here and remind me to wear my coat the next time? How about stopping to help?"

It doesn't matter what words they actually use. The underlying Burning Imperative of every life squad, ambulance team, or first responder of any sort must be *"help people in need."* This life squad captain was not living the message. You must. Be. Do. Say.

Burning Imperative—Summary and Implications

The Burning Imperative is the cornerstone building block of tactical capacity. Everything pivots off a business's mission, vision, objectives, goals, strategies, and values:

- *Headline:* All-encapsulating phrase or tagline
- *Mission:* Why are we here, why do we exist, what business are we in?
- *Vision:* Future picture—what want to become; where going?
- *Objectives:* Broadly defined, *qualitative* performance requirements
- *Goals:* The *quantitative* measures of the objectives that define success

- *Strategies:* Broad choices around *how* the team will achieve its objectives
- *Values:* Beliefs and moral principles that guide attitudes, decisions, and actions

For the Burning Imperative to drive everything everyone actually does every day, it must be truly embraced by all. Thus, you should strive to get it in place and shared early on—within your first 30 days at the latest.

QUESTIONS YOU SHOULD ASK YOURSELF

- Have we laid the right foundation on which to build a high-performing team?
- Have we identified a Burning Imperative?
- Is it compelling enough to the key stakeholders?
- Do we have a strategy and plan to make it real?

TOOL 10.1
Imperative Workshop

This is a one-day, off-site workshop to drive consensus around mission, vision, objectives, goals, strategies, and values. **All** members of the core team must attend. This workshop will determine the team's Burning Imperative.

Preparation

In premeeting communications, set a clear destination for the meeting (mission, vision, objectives, goals, strategies, and values).

Set context—current reality—broader group's purpose.

Send invitations, set logistics.

Prepare to present your current vision (leader); prepare to explain your role (team members).

Delivery

Detail the destination: framework, mission, vision, objectives, goals, strategies, plans, and values (facilitator).

Present the current vision (team leader).

Present the current subgroup roles (team members).

Set up what's important.

Review the corporate/larger-group purpose (team leader).

Revise the team's mission, vision, objectives, goals, strategies, and plans in turn by encouraging an open, but focused discussion to expand ideas. Group them into similar categories, select the ones that resonate with current vision, rank them in order of importance, solicit individual drafts, collect common thoughts, create a group draft based on input that includes the Burning Imperative headline (facilitator).

Discuss how the new Burning Imperative is different from the old situation (facilitator).

Summarize what it will take to achieve the Burning Imperative (facilitator).

Wrap up and tie the results back to the destination and communicate the next steps.

Follow-Up

Share with all team members for input.

Make refinements if required.

Communicate the final results to all key stakeholders.

Exploit Key *Milestones* to Drive Team Performance by Day 45

Part I—**POSITION** and **SELL** yourself; **MAP** and **AVOID** land mines, Do your **DUE DILIGENCE**

M̲ilestones are the building blocks of tactical capacity that turn a Burning Imperative into a manageable action plan. Done right, your team's milestone management practice will be a powerful team reinforcer. *This is all about follow-through.* In brief, drive clarity around:

- Decision rights
- Accountabilities
- Linkages across groups
- Information flows
- Collaboration

Once this is done, move the focus from the individuals to the team.

Follow Through—Or Don't Even Start

Sam's team put a lot of time and energy into creating a Burning Imperative during a two-day workshop. They left excited and ready to move forward. Then Sam got busy and never put the milestone management process in place. As a result, the team quickly went back to doing things the way they'd been doing them before. If Sam wasn't going to follow through, why should they?

The real test of moving from strategy to tactical capacity lies in the actual practices that are set up among team members. Tactical capacity implies, by definition, that significant leeway should be built into practices. A team that has internalized its imperative, mission, values, and objectives will have developed a keen sense of mutually assured success. Having done this, they will have built a real foundation for true tactical capacity, and will do what it takes to succeed, even if that means adapting and modifying aspects of the initial plans that were laid out. There should be nothing mechanical about this aspect of preparing for and executing a complex transition. It requires nuance, insight, close monitoring, and collaboration.

Practices are the things that enable people to implement the plans. They need to be coupled with systems of metrics and rewards that reinforce the desired behaviors. There is an old saying: "Show me how they are paid and I'll tell you what they really do."

John Michael Loh, United States Air Force Air Combat Command during the first Gulf War said: "I used to believe that if it doesn't get measured, it doesn't get done. Now I say if it doesn't get measured it doesn't get approved . . . you need to manage by facts, not gut feel." And as Michael Bloomberg puts it, "You're entitled to your own opinions, but not your own facts."[1]

Specific performance measurements, accountabilities, and decision rights free people and teams to do their jobs without undue interference and provide the basis for nonjudgmental discussion of performance versus expectations and how to make improvements.

---

[1] Michael Bloomberg, University of Pennsylvania Commencement Address, May 2008.

It is essential that people know what is expected of them. Once the expectations are clear, they also must have the time and resources needed to deliver toward those expectations. The milestone management process is focused on clarifying decision rights and making sure information and resources flow to where they need to go.

Milestones Are Checkpoints along the Way to a Defined Goal

Recall these definitions from Chapter 10:

- *Objectives:* Broadly defined, *qualitative* performance requirements
- *Goals:* The *quantitative* measures of the objectives that define success
- *Strategies:* Broad choices around how the team will achieve its objectives

Now add:

- *Milestones: Checkpoints* along the way to achieving objectives and goals

NASA and the Apollo 13 ground team provide a useful example of this. The objective of getting the astronauts back home alive after the explosion in space was compelling, but overwhelming. It was easier to work through milestones one-by-one:

- Turn the ship around so it would get back to earth.
- Manage the remaining power so it would last until they were back.
- Fix the carbon monoxide problem so the air remained breathable.
- Manage reentry into the atmosphere so the ship didn't burn up.

The power of milestones is that they let you know how you're doing along the way and give you the opportunity to make adjustments. They also give you the comfort to let your team run toward the goal without your involvement, as long as the milestones are being reached as planned.

You might evaluate your team's journey to a goal like this:

Worst case	The team misses a goal and doesn't know why.
Bad	The team misses a goal and knows why.
Okay	The team misses a milestone but adjusts to make the overall goal.
Good	The team *anticipates risk as it goes along to make key milestones*.
Best	The team hits all milestones on the way to goal . . . (in your dreams).

Imagine you set a goal of getting from London to Paris in 5½ hours. Now imagine that you choose to drive. Imagine further that it takes you 45 minutes to get from Central London to the outskirts of London.

How's the trip going so far?

You have no clue.

You might be on track. You might be behind schedule. But it's early in the trip so you probably think you can make up time later if you need to. So you're not worried.

If, on the other hand, you had set the following milestones, you would be thinking differently:

- Central London to outskirts of London: 30 minutes
- Outskirts of London to Folkstone: 70 minutes
- Channel Crossing: load: 20 minutes; cross: 20 minutes; unload: 20 minutes
- Calais to Paris: 3 hours

If you had set a milestone of getting to the outskirts of London in 30 minutes and it took you 45 minutes, you would know you were behind schedule. Knowing that you were behind schedule, you could then take action on alternative options. The milestone would make you immediately aware of the need to adjust to still reach your overall goal.

You and your team are going to miss milestones. It is not necessary to hit all your milestones. What is essential is that you and your team have put in place a mechanism to identify reasonable milestones so you have checkpoints that allow you to anticipate and adjust along the way.

Manage Milestone Updates with a Three-Step Process

Deploying a mutually supportive team-based follow-up system helps everyone improve performance versus goals. Organizations that have deployed this process in their team meetings have seen dramatic improvements in team performance. Follow these three steps as well as the prep and post instructions laid out here and in Tool 11.1.

Prep: Circulate individual milestone updates to the team to read before each meeting so you can take update sharing and reporting off the agenda, while still deploying a disciplined process to make sure information flows where it needs to go.

1. *Use the first half of each meeting for each team member to headline wins, learning, and areas in which the person needs help from other team members,* but do not work through items at this point. Working items here reinforces a "first-come, first-serve" mentality where the people who share later in the order tend to get squeezed for time.

2. *Pause at the halfway point of the meeting to prioritize items for discussion* so the team can discuss items in the right priority order instead of first-come, first-serve. These won't necessarily be the universally most important items since some items should be worked with a different group or subset of the team. Instead, these will be the most important items for this team to work *as a team* at this time.

3. *Use the second half of the meeting to discuss the overall team's most important issues and opportunities* with regard to milestone delivery in priority order. The expectation is that the team won't get through all the items. That's okay because you're working the most important items first. (Which is why you paused to prioritize items.) This is the time to figure out how to adjust *as a team*

to make the most important goals, all the while reinforcing pre-determined decision rights.

Post: Defer other items to the next meeting or a separate meeting.

Hot Tip I

Anticipation is the key: At first, milestones will go from "on track" to "oops we missed" with no steps in between. You'll know the process is working well when people are surfacing areas they "might miss" if they don't get help from others. Focus your love and attention on these "might miss" items to get the team to help so people feel good about surfacing them and look forward to bringing them to the group for help.

Hot Tip II

Banish "first-come, first-serve": This milestone process is easy to deploy for disciplined people and teams. It is hard for less disciplined people because they want to work items "first-come, first-serve." Resist that. Follow the process. You'll learn to love it. (Well, maybe not love it, but you will appreciate it. It will strengthen your team.)

Hot Tip III

Integrate across instead of managing down: The milestone meetings are great forums for making connections across groups. The further you rise in the organization, the more time you'll spend integrating across and the less time you'll spend managing down. Senior managers don't like to be managed from above or have their decision rights compromised, but everyone appreciates improved information flows and linking projects and priorities across groups.

Use Milestone Management at the Board Level

Garr's board meetings were out of control. Individual board members kept taking the group off the meetings' agendas to emphasize their own favorite issues.

To combat this, Garr put in place a milestone management process.

Each board member submitted his or her updates to the board secretary ahead of the board meeting. The secretary then compiled them and sent them back to everyone at least 48 hours in advance of the board meetings.

At the two-hour board meetings, the first hour was spent with each of the 24 board members giving a two-minute recap of their updates, emphasizing the areas where they needed help or thought more discussion was warranted.

At the halfway point, the board president, looked at all the outstanding issues and ordered them from highest priority to lowest priority.

The board spent the next hour working through the issues in priority order, not worrying about time. They never got through the entire list in the meetings. But that was okay because the issues they got to were more important than the issues that had to be discussed later.

This revolutionized the board meetings. Everyone got two minutes in the spotlight. Everyone got a chance to raise issues. But the agenda was no longer managed on a first-come, first-serve basis. As a result, the board could spend more time on the more important issues.

Milestones—Summary and Implications

Tracking milestones is not a revolutionary idea. For most, the idea of using the way you manage milestones as a way to build the team is new.

1. Get milestones in place.
2. Track them and manage them *as a team*.

Prep: Circulate updates in advance of meetings.

- Share wins, learning, and areas for help (might miss) in first half of meeting.
- Prioritize items.
- Work items in priority order in second half of meeting.

Post: Defer other items to next meeting or separate meeting.

QUESTIONS YOU SHOULD ASK YOURSELF

- Is everyone clear on who (roles) is doing what (goals), when (milestones), with what resources and decision rights?
- Are we doing all we can to make sure information and resources flow to where they need to go?
- Is there a system in place to manage milestone achievement so I do not have to do it myself on an ad hoc basis?

Milestones Management Process*

—Leader conducts a weekly or biweekly Milestones Management meeting with his/her team.

—Prior to Milestones Management meetings:

Each team member submits updates.

Designated person compiles and circulates updated milestones in advance of the meeting.

—At Milestones Management meetings:

First half of meeting

Each team member gives a five-minute update in the following format—most important wins, most important learnings, areas where he/she needs help.

Midpoint of meeting

The leader orders topics for discussion in order of priority.

Second half of meeting

Group discusses priority topics in order, spending as much time as necessary on each topic.

The remaining topics are deferred to the next Milestones Management meeting or a separate meeting.

(continued)

Downloadable TOOL 11.1   (continued)

Milestones Tracking

Milestones	Who	When	Status*	Learning	Help Needed
Priority Programs					
Capabilities					

*Status possibilities: On track; Lagging but will be made up; Heading for a miss.

Overinvest in *Early Wins* to Build Team Confidence by Day 60

Part I—**POSITION** and **SELL** yourself; **MAP** and **AVOID** land mines, Do your **DUE DILIGENCE**

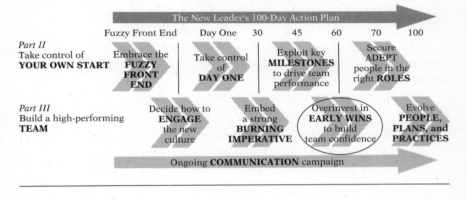

T here is often a conversation about six months after a leader has started a new role. Someone will ask the new leader's boss how the new leader is doing. You have probably taken part in these conversations before.

"By the way, how's that new leader Rhonda doing?"

"Rhonda? She's fabulous. Love the intelligence. Love the attitude. She may be off to a slow start. But what a great hire! Really like her."

Result: Rhonda's probably on the way out; or, at the very least, in real trouble. Rhonda may not find out about it for another 6 to 12 months but her boss's "off to a slow start" planted a seed of doubt that could eventually lead to an unhappy ending for Rhonda.

After all, senior leaders are hired to deliver results first and foremost, and it is assumed that the required intelligence, personality, and attitude come along with the package. So when that question is asked about your transition, you want the answer to be about specific results, or early wins.

Compare the previous answer with "Rhonda? Let me tell you about all the things she's gotten done."

In that scenario, Rhonda's made. Of course, she has not done it all herself. Her team has. But Rhonda got the team focused on delivering early wins and by doing so gave her boss something concrete to talk about.

Early wins give the leader *credibility* and provide the team *confidence* and *momentum*—three very good things. For NASA and Apollo 13, fixing the oxygen problem was the early win that made the entire team believe they could succeed and gave them the confidence to deal with the rest of their challenges and the momentum to push forward despite incredible odds.

Our early win prescription is relatively simple:

1. Select one or two early wins from your milestones list:
   - Choose early wins that will make a meaningful external impact.
   - Select early wins that your boss will want to talk about.
   - Pick early wins that you are sure you can deliver.
   - Choose early wins that will model important behaviors.
   - Pick early wins that would not have happened if you had not been there.
2. Establish early wins in your second month and deliver by your sixth month:
   - Early means early. Make sure you select early wins in your first 60 days that you and the team can deliver by the end of your sixth month. Select them early. Communicate them early. Deliver them early.
   - Make sure the team understands the early wins and has bought in to delivering them on time.
   - This will give your bosses the concrete results they need when someone asks how you are doing.

3. Overinvest resources toward early wins to overdeliver:

   • Do not skimp on your early wins. Allocate resources in a manner that will ensure timely delivery. Put more resources than you think you should need against these early opportunities so your team is certain to deliver them better and faster than anyone thought was possible.

   • Stay alert. Adjust quickly. As the leader, stay close and stay involved on the progress of your early wins and react immediately if they start to fall even slightly off track or behind schedule.

4. Celebrate and communicate early wins:

   • As your first early wins are achieved, celebrate the accomplishment with the entire team. This is important and should not be overlooked.

   • In conjunction with your communication campaign, make sure your early wins are communicated as appropriate.

In general, "early wins" are not synonymous with "big wins." They are the early, sometimes small, yet meaningful wins that start the momentum of a winning team. They are the blasting caps, not the dynamite. They are the opening singles, not the grand-slam home run. They are the first successful test market, not the global expansion. They are generally found by accelerating something that is already in progress instead of starting something new. They are sure to generate credibility, confidence, momentum, and excitement.

Don't Wait Too Long to Build Momentum

Rudy Giuliani went into the 2007/2008 campaign for the Republican nomination for president of the United States as the early favorite, leading the national polls by a substantial margin. He put virtually all his effort into winning the first big primary in Florida to build momentum going into "super Tuesday" when half the states would hold primaries. In doing this, he chose to skip the earlier, smaller states like Iowa and New Hampshire.

Before the Florida primary, when the political pundits were asked about Rudy Giuliani, his strategy left them with nothing to say, while several of the other candidates had tangible results to speak to.

Rudy took himself out of the debate precisely because he had no results to talk about. The other candidates positioned themselves at the top of the headlines for weeks and developed confidence and momentum that rose to counteract Giuliani's early lead. His win big strategy backfired because it took too long to deliver tangible results and it led to a disastrous third-place finish in Florida that forced him out of the race.

Focus on the Results with the Most Impact

Pamela came into lead sales and marketing for a struggling software provider. Pamela knew that the product was very strong and well priced, but the company had little market penetration due to its less than stellar marketing efforts. Immediately on joining, Pamela, with her team, did a nice job of getting the imperative and milestones in place. Then it was time to pick an early win. Her team's important milestones included redoing the marketing strategy, positioning, branding, brochures, and a new trade show booth. As an early win, she and the team picked redesigning the trade show booth and the trade shows strategy. Her logic was that there was a major trade show coming up in a few months and this was a great chance to make a powerful impact on the market. She knew that if the team was successful, the end result would be a significant increase in client interest and inquiries. If she could increase client requests for proposals, she knew fortunes would turn around because the sales team had an excellent close ratio once they got on a client's radar. By generating more client requests, she knew she would gain credibility for the marketing group, gain confidence for her team, and give senior management some meaningful results to talk about.

She closely managed the project while effectively engaging her team along the way and delivered a superior product in record time. Pam's team came up with a concept that attracted key clients and then blew them away once they were there. The sales team gave more presentations during the trade show than they had in the previous eight months. Her team's early win generated tangible, effective, and exciting results. It was far better than what they had achieved before and clearly something they never would have accomplished without Pamela. It was a great early win!

Champion the Champions

Oscar decided to focus his efforts on four projects. He reached into his organization to pick four "champions" to drive the projects and then gave them extra support and resources onboarding into their new roles.

Three of the projects produced early tangible results. One did not do so well.

But the three that did well were enough to turn the whole business around. The division Oscar had been brought in to run had been declining 1 percent every month for 24 months, as it did for Oscar's first two months. Then, in month three, it was up 1 percent. In month four, it was up 4 percent. In month five, it was up 10 percent. Also, the overwhelming success of the three early wins bought Oscar more time to achieve a win on the fourth.

No one even bothered asking how Oscar was doing in month six. Everybody knew because the numbers told the story.

Redefine Success

When we presented the idea to Quincy, he did not like the early win concept at all. He had just become the new head of the music division of a major entertainment company that was looking to make a dramatic impact on the music industry and turn around years of declining sales. Quincy knew that the existing pipeline of artists could not deliver the sales punch that his bosses were looking for, and he was certain that it would take 12 to 18 months to deliver anything tangible. To him, delivering a meaningful early win in his first six months seemed impossible.

So, we helped him rethink how he defined early wins. He borrowed the pipeline concept from pharmaceutical companies and created a recording pipeline. On Day One, the pipeline was near empty. But, by month six he had an exciting array of new artists signed and viable projects in the pipeline and could show senior management the new face of the music division as his measure of success. His early win was showing tangible momentum toward a longer-term goal.

Hot Tip

Overinvest in early wins: This is the key to dealing with the early delivery land mine. You never have as much time as you think. It usually takes more resources than you think. Getting an early win is about survival for the new leader and renewed confidence for the team. It is that important. So overinvest in it accordingly.

Charter the Team for the Early Win

It is essential that the early win create a sense of confidence and momentum in the team that can only happen when the team drives the win. You, as the leader, can inspire and enable by directing, supporting, and encouraging the team in the process; but it can't be your win. It must be the team's win. Therefore, your role as leader is to set the team up for success and support its efforts. The team charter and its five core components are useful in doing that. They are laid out here and in Tool 12.1.

1. *Objective*—What?
   - Clearly and specifically define the early win.
   - Use the SMART goal format to specifically define the early win and the required goals along the way.
   - The goals must generate tangible results as detailed in the early wins prescription previously described.
2. *Context*—Why?
   - Provide the *information* that led to objectives—especially customer requirements.
   - Explain your *intent* so people on the team can understand the collective *purpose* of their discrete *tasks* and adjust along the way to achieve that purpose while minimizing unintended consequences.
   - Clarify what happens next—the *follow-on actions* to ensure that momentum is sustained after the win is delivered.

3. *Resources*—With what help?

   - Ensure the team has and can access all the *human, financial, and operational* resources needed to deliver the objective. (Remember, for an early win, you're going to overinvest in resources to ensure delivery.)

   - Clarify what *other teams,* groups, units are involved and what their roles are.

   - Allocate resources in a timely manner to ensure delivery.

4. *Guidelines*—How?

   - Clarify what the team can and cannot do with regard to *roles* and *decisions*.

   - Lay out the *interdependencies* between the team being chartered and the other teams involved.

   - Decide what essential data is needed to measure results.

   - Provide frequent and easy access to required data.

5. *Accountability*—Track and Monitor

   - Clarify what is going to get done by when by whom and how the team and you are going to track *milestones* so you can know about risks in advance and can intervene well before milestones are missed.

   - Clarify *command, communication, and support* arrangements so everyone knows how they are going to work together.

   - Schedule regular updates.

   - Know the signs when course corrections or reevaluations are necessary.

Overinvest in Early Wins—Summary and Implications

Early wins are all about credibility, confidence, and momentum. People have more faith in people who have delivered. You want your boss to have confidence in you. You want the team to have confidence in you and in themselves. Early wins will provide that confidence.

QUESTIONS YOU SHOULD ASK YOURSELF

- Have I identified an early win that will accomplish all that it needs to in terms of securing my job and giving the team confidence?
- Do I have confidence in the team's strategy and tactical capacity to deliver this win?
- Am I certain that I have invested enough resources to accomplish the win?

Team Charter Worksheet*

Useful for getting teams off to the best start on their way to an early win.

Objectives/Goals: Charge the team with delivering specific, measurable results (SMART).

_____

_____

_____

_____

Context: Information that led to objectives?

_____

_____

_____

Intent behind the objectives?

_____

_____

What's going to happen after the objective is achieved?

_____

_____

_____

_____

Resources: Human, financial, and operational resources available to the team. Other teams, groups, units working in parallel, supporting, or interdependent areas.

_____

_____

_____

_____

Guidelines: Clarify what the team can and cannot do with regard to *roles* and *decisions*. Lay out the *interdependencies* between the team being chartered and the other teams involved.

_____

_____

_____

_____

(continued)

Downloadable TOOL 12.1   (continued)

Accountability: Be clear on accountability structure, update timing, and completion timing.

_____

_____

_____

_____

_____

CHAPTER 13

Secure *ADEPT* People in the Right Roles with the Right Support by Day 70

Part I—**POSITION** and **SELL** yourself; **MAP** and **AVOID** land mines, Do your **DUE DILIGENCE**

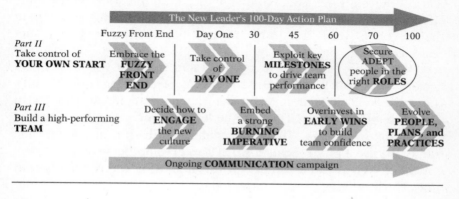

O f all the tools in your toolbox, putting people in the right roles is one of the most powerful. It is also the most explosive. As you seek to Evolve (or Shock!) the culture, these moves will be the most decisive and will have the greatest impact.

Often, team members of a culture or organization that is beginning to evolve will watch and wait to see if there are any consequences for not evolving with the new culture. They will pay particular attention to the team members who say things like, "All that meeting and report stuff is fine, but if it means I have to change what I do, forget it!" The moment somebody is terminated or moved or promoted, those who have been resisting the change often develop a completely different view of things.

Everybody on the team feels it when people moves are made. Everyone will have an opinion (usually strong) on the moves and how they affect them. Personnel moves spark emotions, fears, and egos, so you need to be careful and thoughtful about who, what, and especially when you move people. Recognize that moving people should actually be seen as your most potent communication tool: this woman means business and she means it now!

As a leader, you can help your team and the people you're working with see their roles in a more comprehensive light if you make an effort to link it directly to their career development. Many people are not in the right role for the team's mission or even for their own professional development. Moving roles is often as much about doing what is right for the individual as it is for the team. If you can develop the leadership skill of communicating with people effectively about roles and careers, you will be investing not only in the success of your first 100 Days, but in your own long-term success as a leader.

When it comes to sorting people and roles on your team, you need to work with a short-term and a long-term framework. Initially, you must look at your team to determine what, if any short-term moves should be made. Then, in the longer term, you must continue to monitor your team. This chapter deals with the short-term time frame. We use a process called ADEPT to develop the team over time. Appendix V gives you a context for this and ideas you can apply over time. The headlines are:

Acquire	Scope roles.
	Identify prospects.
	Recruit and select the right people for the right roles.
	Attract those people.
	Onboard them so they can deliver better results faster.
Develop	Assess performance drivers.
	Develop skills and knowledge for current and future roles.
Encourage	Provide clear direction, objectives, measures, etc.
	Support with the resources and time required for success.

	Reinforce desired behaviors with recognition and rewards.
Plan	Monitor peoples' performance over time.
	Assess their situation and potential.
	Plan career moves/succession planning over time.
Transition	Migrate people to different roles to fit their needs/life stage, and company needs.

Start by making sure you've got the right people in the right roles. It's unlikely you'll acquire a team that is perfectly set up to deliver against your Burning Imperative. If you're lucky, with a couple of small tweaks you'll be on your way to a world-class team! However, depending on the amount of change that you are trying to drive, you may need to do a major overhaul. If so, be prepared for a lot of work and a lot of dislocation. The earlier you make that assessment the better. Don't make the mistake of delaying or avoiding the people changes that need to be made while hoping against hope that some magical transformation will occur. It won't.

We push hard on this issue. Often we make our clients feel uncomfortable by suggesting they make people moves faster than they've been used to doing. For some reason, it is human nature to put off such decisions off. We have a strong bias for figuring them out as early as possible and making the moves quickly. It is hard medicine for most people to swallow, but it's much like a child's fear of pulling off a Band-Aid quickly. Once it is removed, the child realizes the process was not so very painful after all. Get this process done quickly—you'll be happy you did. You certainly do not have to follow our advice on timing, but we strongly suggest that you do. Getting the right people in the right roles with the right support is a fundamental, essential building block of a high-performing team. Without the right people in the right roles, there is no team.

Getting ADEPT people in the right roles is guided by the team's mission, vision, and values, as well as by individuals' strengths. The mission determines the ideal organization—what roles are required to do the things that need to be done on a daily basis. This gives you a map of the roles you need to have—and the roles you do not need.

Southwest Airlines is in the business of transporting people by airplane. Their organization needs to include people to maintain the planes, fly the planes, sell tickets, and serve their passengers. They need these roles. They do not need chefs, bartenders, or masseuses—even though some other airlines do have people in those roles.

With a picture of required roles in hand, you can now look at which roles will have the greatest impact on achieving your vision. The roles responsible for these tasks are the critical ones. The other roles encompass tasks that can be done merely "good enough." This is where strategy and people overlap—determining which roles need to be best in class and invested in, and which roles can be just maintained or outsourced.

The airline industry, as an industry, loses buckets of money over the long-term. (This is true for most industries centered on transporting people.) Yet, Southwest makes money every year. Part of why they do is that they have figured out which are their critical roles. Southwest overinvests in maintenance roles so they can turn their planes around faster. They overinvest in training their stewardesses and stewards so passengers' in-air experience is fun. Conversely, they underinvest in food service and on-the-ground waiting spaces.

The NASA team members on Apollo 13 were aligned around a clear Burning Imperative, had clear milestones, and got an early win by fixing the oxygen/carbon-monoxide problem. While everyone was willing to do whatever it took to get the astronauts home safely, they stayed in their roles. One group of physicists figured out how to wrap the spacecraft around the moon and get it going in the right direction. Another group of engineers fixed the oxygen problem. Another group dealt with the reentry calculations. The spare crew truly did whatever it took to try things out. They were all working together without getting in each other's way.

Strengths

Now, you are ready to match the right people with the right roles. Marcus Buckingham and Don Clifton's[1] core premise is that people do better when they capitalize on their own, individual *strengths*—talent, knowledge, and skills.

Strengths are necessary for success. But they are not sufficient. People must want to do well and they must fit in. It is helpful to think in terms of strengths, motivation, and fit.

---

[1]Marcus Buckingham and Donald Clifton, *Now Discover Your Strengths* (New York: Free Press, 2001).

Motivation

You did your own work on your values and goals as part of the Five-Step Career Plan (Tool 1.1). As a leader, you need to do a similar kind of work with your team. If you understand their values, their goals, and how they see what they are currently doing in light of those goals, you have a terrific advantage in helping them find or live up to the right role for themselves and for the organization.

Fit

Fit comes out of perspective, values, and biases. Perspective, in turn, comes out of how people have been trained to view and solve business problems. This is the accumulation of people's business experience as manifested in their mental models. People with a classic sales perspective may feel they can sell any product to customers. Conversely, people with more of a marketing perspective may feel the organization should modify its products and services to meet customers' needs. We are not suggesting that one perspective is better than the other, just that they are different.

We talked about values in Chapter 10, when discussing the Burning Imperative. It is rare for all of any individual's values to match all of the organization's values. However, it is important for most of the core values to match and for none of them to be in direct conflict with each other.

Different people work in different ways. Some roles may require people with a greater sense of urgency. Some roles require people who think things through thoroughly before jumping in. If someone who tends to get a later start on the day is assigned the role of making morning coffee for the group before everyone else comes in, it would force the person to work in opposition to a natural bias and would most likely be a recipe for failure (and bad coffee).

Don't Wait

It is a classic tale. It was Game 7 of the 2003 American League Baseball Championship Series. The winner moved on to the World Series. The New York Yankees, perennial winners and their pitching ace Roger Clemens versus the Boston Red Sox with 86 years of disappointment and their pitching ace Pedro Martinez.

Fourth inning: Clemens is struggling. Yankee manager Joe Torre takes him out—early, decisively, without a lot of discussion.

Eighth inning: Martinez is struggling. Red Sox manager Grady Little goes out to the pitcher's mound and asks if Martinez has "enough bullets in (his) tank." The response: "I have enough." Little leaves him in. "Pedro wanted to stay in there," Little said. "He wanted to get the job done, just as he has many times for us all season long." As Martinez put it, "I would never say no. I tried hard and I did whatever possible to win the ballgame."

Martinez and the Red Sox proceed to blow the lead and lose the game. Once again Clemens, Torre and the Yankees go on to the World Series while two weeks later, Little loses his job.

As the sportswriters put it, Little's decision was "based more on loyalty and emotion than logic." From Torre's point of view, "In Game 7, you've got a short leash. I'd worry about his emotions after the game."

There is a lot in common between Game 7 and a complex transition. Everyone is on a short leash. So it's essential to move early and decisively.

Don't Let One Bad Apple Spoil the Batch

Charlie was the new head of the division. One of his direct reports, Jim, was deploying blatantly passive-aggressive tactics to undermine Charlie's authority. On a regular basis, Jim would:

- Sit in the back of large meetings and carrying on side conversations during Charlie's presentations.
- Refuse to work on the agreed divisional priorities until he and his team had completed their annual plans presentation.
- Refuse to do prework for Charlie's meetings because he didn't think the process was meaningful.

We had a tough conversation with Charlie about this: "You need to get Jim off your team."

"Can't do it. My boss put Jim in place and has a lot of confidence in him."

"If you move on Jim, your boss will think less of you, will think you didn't give Jim a chance, will think less of you as a manager. If you do not move on Jim, you will get fired within six months because Jim is going to make sure your team does not work."

Charlie moved on Jim. Six months later, Charlie's boss was moved aside (and took Jim with him.)

This story and the story of the Yankees beating the Red Sox in the American League Championship Series make the same point. You have to do what is right for the organization *and* what's right for the individuals. You have to find a way to get the right people in the right roles at the right time. You have to do it early and decisively. You should worry about their emotions—but never let them interfere with making the right decisions at the right time.

Keep People in the Right Roles

When Bamkanai was promoted to head up another division, Iris took his spot as the CEO. Of all the people on her team, Jamil, the head of technology, was her favorite. Incredibly intelligent, great people skills, completely, but completely, reliable. That team spun like a top.

So she appointed Jamil chief operating officer (COO), got the current COO to go join Bamkanai in his division (a masterful move she thought), and promoted the number two technology person to the top spot. Those first meetings were so great for Iris! What a team! But two things happened. Jamil was totally unaccustomed to the more consensual decision making of senior management and struggled to adjust. Meanwhile, the number two, Gahim, made several terrible mistakes, including not telling Jamil, who was very distracted, about them.

Bad choice. It was a painful retrenchment, but Iris managed to get Jamil to where he should have been all along, head of technology, and found a seasoned COO to run companywide operations. Two years later, Jamil once again had the opportunity to step up. This time he, and the technology team, were up to the move.

Once you have people in the right role, leave them there and support them in that role. Also, remember that just because someone is good in one role doesn't mean they'll be good in another role that requires different strengths and motivations.

Cut the Pain Out Early

Connie had never been sure of Andrew. She was going to make a decision about him in "due time." Then Andrew turned to a facilitator at one of Connie's meetings during the break and said, "You should know I don't trust Connie. I think she screwed me out of a promotion and is out to get me."

There is an old adage that you cannot trust someone who doesn't trust you. Connie's due time had arrived.

Cut the Pain Out Early (or, at Least, as Early as Practical)

Sherman had just taken over as general manager. He knew he had to improve both the sales and marketing functions dramatically, as soon as he could. To achieve that, he knew he had to replace the heads of both functions; but he also knew that both were extremely valuable, respected, and valued employees who could make important contributions in other roles that would better leverage their strengths, motivation, and fit.

What Sherman did, that still seems to have made sense, was to begin recruiting for their replacements immediately, while building strong personal relationships with them and working to figure out other roles for them.

Fast-forward six months. Sherman put a new heads of sales and marketing in place. He kept the old heads of sales and marketing as direct reports, but he put them in new, more appropriate roles that enabled them to make an important impact on the organization and actively help their replacements succeed.

How Fast Should You Move on the Team?

In general, we suggest having your plan in place to sort roles and make people moves at the end of 70 days or 10 weeks. There will be times when you need to move much faster, and there will be times when it will take you longer to implement the plan but the 70th day is a good target time frame to have it all figured out.

There is a risk in moving too fast. The risk is that you'll make poor decisions and come across as too impulsive. By the 70th day, you will have had a chance to see people in the imperative workshop, in the milestone management process and, some of them, in the early win kickoff. At the 70th day, you should be able to make your decisions based on past reports and on your own observations. Thus, for making decisions on most of your team, 70 days won't seem too fast.

There's a larger risk in moving too slow. At about 100 days, you own the team. Once you own the team, the problem children become your problem children. You can't blame the team's failings or unresolved issues on your predecessor any more. Also, the other team members know who the weak links are and they might have known since before you took the helm. The number-one thing high performers want is for management to act on low performers so the whole group can do better.[2] If you move too slowly, the other team members will wonder what took you so long.

To be clear, you may not be able to implement your decisions all at once. You may need to put in place transition plans that support weaker team members or keep strong team members in the wrong roles during the time it takes to get their replacements on board and up to speed. We're not suggesting you make all your moves in your first 70 days, no matter what. We are suggesting you have the plan in place and begin making moves as appropriate and that you do so with a bias toward making the moves sooner rather than later.

HOT TIP

Move faster on the team: Have a bias to move faster on your team than you think you should. The risks of moving too fast are nothing compared with the multiplier effect of leaving people in the wrong place too long.

Map Performance and Role

Putting the right people in the right roles is a key driver of success. The heart of Tool 13.1 is a grid that matches people with roles. The grid is based on two dimensions: performance and role appropriateness. Mapping people on this grid then helps inform decisions about which people are in the right roles and which are in the wrong so you can support some and move others. This is a simple but highly effective tool for thinking about a complex subject.[3]

---

[2] Thank you Dave Kuhlman of Sibson Consulting for this insight.
[3] Note this is different than Drotter's 9-box tool that crosses performance and potential. The 9-box helps you think about future promotions. This 4-box matrix of performance and fit with the role helps you think about whether people are in the right role now.

Keep in mind that some people may be in the wrong role precisely because they have outgrown it and are ready for a promotion. If you leave those type of people in their roles you'll face a growing motivation risk. Another person may find themselves in the wrong role if they are working like crazy to make up for a mismatch between their strengths and those required for the job. The "Evolve" box is the appropriate place for those people. In either situation, you can clearly see the value of having a plan to move each candidate to a more appropriate role. Delay those moves and you'll find yourself and your team in trouble.

FIGURE 13.1   Performance versus Role Match

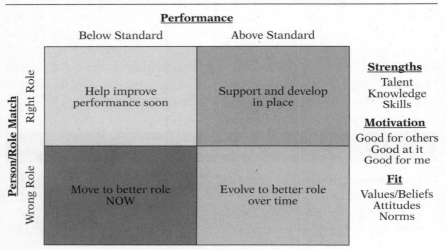

Performance versus Role Match

In general, the suggested actions from Figure 13.1 are:

- *Support:* Right Role/Above Standard: Keep in current roles. Support and develop them. These people are helping and will continue to help. Make sure to push their ability to do good for others and for themselves as high as possible.

- *Improve:* Right Role/Below Standard: Invest to improve these people's performance. They can deliver with the right direction, training, and support.

- *Evolve:* Wrong Role/Above Standard: Actively look for better fit before performance drops. Resist the temptation to keep in current role. They are helping, but the potential exists for even more.

- *Move:* Wrong Role/Below Standard: Move to a better role inside or outside the team—*immediately.*

The Performance measure is drawn from an individual's last or current review/assessment in their current role. It is driven by results versus goals and supplemented with recently observed performance, behaviors, and communication.

The Role Match measure is a correlation of the strengths, motivations, and fit required for the role compared with the strengths, motivations, and fit of the person filling that role. The role's strengths, motivations, and fit should be drawn from position descriptions. The individual's strengths, motivations, and fit could be drawn from their latest review, Gallup's StrengthFinder™, or another assessment questionnaire or tool.

Mapping performance and role appropriateness facilitates a more urgent identification of who is in the right role and who is in the wrong role now. It is important not to confuse "role match" with "potential" because there is a significant difference between the two.

Potential gets at future promotions. What is required to help people move up the ladder? What is the appropriate time line for those promotions?

Role match gets at the current position. What's the likelihood of their performing well in their current position?

Every organization has its own way of doing position profiles. The better profiles include the key elements of the mission, strengths, motivation, and fit. One way to do this is to answer the following questions in each of the following areas:

Mission

- What is the mission for this position? Why does it exist?
- What are the responsibilities associated with the role?
- What are the desired objectives or outcomes of the position?
- What impact should the role have on the rest of organization?

Strengths

- What *talents* are required to achieve success in the role? (Consider talents to be a recurring pattern of thoughts, feelings, or behavior that can be productively applied.)

- What *skills* are required to achieve success in the role? (Consider skills as the "how-to's," or the steps of an activity. They can also be identified as capabilities that can be transferred such as technical, interpersonal, or business skills.)
- What *knowledge* is required to achieve success in the role? (Consider what the role holder need be aware of or know. What are the required education, experience, and qualifications?)[4]

Motivation

- How do the activities of the role fit with the person's likes, dislikes, and idea job criteria?
- How will the person progress toward the long-term goal? What will drive him or keep her focused?

Fit

- Do the person's values fit the team's?
- Does the person's style and character fit well with the company or team's style and characteristics?
- Does the person's style and character mesh with the supervisor's working style and characteristics?

Secure ADEPT People in the Right Roles—Summary and Implications

Put in place ADEPT organizational processes to Acquire, Develop, Encourage, Plan, and Transition talent over time.

Mission informs the ideal organization and helps identify the required roles.

The vision helps identify which roles are required to be best in class.

Match performance, strengths, motivation, and fit of individuals and roles:

- *Support* and develop high performers in right roles.
- *Improve* performance of low performers in right roles.

---

[4] The strengths definitions are drawn from Buckingham and Clifton's *Now Discover Your Strengths* (New York: Free Press, 2001).

- *Evolve* high performers in wrong role to better roles over time.
- *Move* low performers in wrong role to a better role now.

Some of your most painful choices are going to be in this area. This is one of those areas where trying to please everybody will lead to pleasing nobody. Choosing to act on people who are in the wrong roles now or will soon be in the wrong roles is generally not the most enjoyable part of leadership. But it is an essential part.

QUESTIONS YOU SHOULD ASK YOURSELF

- Am I moving at the right speed to get the right people in the right roles?
- Do I have appropriate backup and contingency plans?
- Do I have the right organizational processes in place for the longer term?

Downloadable TOOL 13.1

Performance/Role Match Grid*

Performance versus Role Match

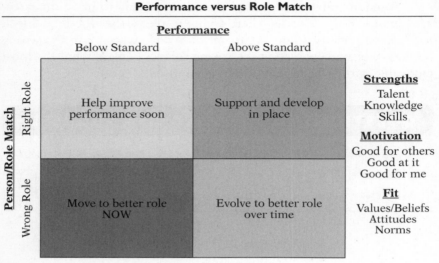

*Copyright © PrimeGenesis® LLC. To customize this document, download Tool 13.1 from www.onboarding-tools.com. The document can then be opened, edited, and printed using Microsoft Word or other word processing applications.

People Actions

Right Role/Above Standard

Keep in current roles. Support and develop them. These people are helping and will continue to help. Make sure to push their ability to do good for others and for themselves as high as possible.

Right Role/Below Standard

Invest to improve performance. They can deliver with the right direction, training, and support.

Wrong Role/Above Standard

Actively look for better fit before performance drops. Resist the temptation to keep in current role. They are helping, but the potential exists for even more.

Wrong Role/Below Standard

Move to a better role inside or outside the team—**immediately**.

Evolve *People*, *Plans*, and *Practices* to Capitalize on Changing Circumstances

Part I—**POSITION** and **SELL** yourself; **MAP** and **AVOID** land mines, Do your **DUE DILIGENCE**

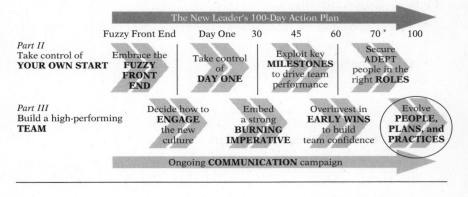

T he 100-day mark is a good moment to start thinking about how you are going to evolve your people, plans, and practices over time to capitalize on changing circumstances. It's useful to set up a predictable rhythm. This allows people to spend less time worrying about the process and more time figuring out how to react and capitalize on the inevitable changes around them. You probably won't be surprised to learn that we think people—plans—practices is a good framework for doing just that.

Capitalizing on Inevitable Changes

Following are important elements to consider on a regular basis.

People

Succession Planning

- Align the longer-term organizational development plans with the longer-term (three-plus year) strategic plan.
- Do this on an annual basis.

Performance Management and Talent Review (One-Year Horizon, Run Annually)

- Track progress of the longer-term succession plan and the corresponding talent needs.
- Do this on an annual basis.

Plans

Strategic Review, Refresh, and Plan

- Conduct a detailed long-term look at the business (three-year horizon), leading to choices around how to create and allocate resources over that longer-term horizon.
- Do this on an annual basis.

Operational Review, Refresh, and Plan

- Ensure that the right operational plans (one-year horizon) are in place that will enable you to deliver the next year's goals.
- Do this on an annual basis.

Practices

Business Reviews and Plan Updates

- Track progress in the context of the operational plan (one-year horizon) and make midcourse adjustments along the way.
- Do this quarterly.

Milestone Updates and Adjustment

- Track the monthly milestones to keep the team focused on the most important things—as a team.
- Do this monthly.

Thinking about these things with these horizons allows you to have a good balance between long-term thinking and short-term execution. A number of our clients have blended these into an annual/quarterly/monthly meeting schedule. The idea is to have a meeting every month with time added once each quarter to deal with longer-term issues. It is a cycle with each piece feeding into the next. Use this calendar as a starting point and then adjust it to meet your organizational needs without dropping any key pieces:

Quarter	Month	Schedule
1	1	Milestone update and adjustment
1	2	**Business review and adjustment/Talent reviews**
1	3	Milestone update and adjustment
2	1	Milestone update and adjustment
2	2	**Business review and adjustment/Strategic review and planning**
2	3	Milestone update and adjustment
3	1	Milestone update and adjustment
3	2	**Business review and adjustment/Succession planning**
3	3	Milestone update and adjustment
4	1	Milestone update and adjustment
4	2	**Business review and adjustment/Operational review and planning**
4	3	Milestone update and adjustment

Adjust to the Inevitable Surprises

John Wooden, the legendary coach of UCLA basketball, whose teams won an astounding 10 NCAA Championships, said: "Things turn out the best for the people who make the best of the way things turn out."

As a leader, it is up to you to make the best of how things turn out. No matter how well you have planned your transition over the first 100 days, no matter how disciplined you are in your follow-up, some things will be different than you expected. Often your ability to keep moving forward while reacting to the unexpected or the unplanned will be the determining factor whether your transition is deemed a success or failure.

One of the main advantages to starting early and deploying the building blocks of tactical capacity quickly is that you and your team will be ready that much sooner to adjust to changing circumstances and surprises. Remember, the ability to respond flexibly and fluidly is a hallmark of a team with tactical capacity. The preceding annual/quarterly/monthly meeting schedule will enable your team to recognize and react to the changes that might impact your team over time.

Not all surprises are equal. Your first job is to sort them out to guide your own and your team's response. If it is a temporary, minor blip, keep your team focused on its existing priorities. If it is minor, but enduring, factor it into your ongoing people, plans, and practices evolution.

Major surprises are a different game. If they're temporary, you'll want to move into crisis or incident management. If they're enduring, you'll need to react and make some fundamental changes to deal with the new reality. When you're evaluating change, use Chart 14.1 to help guide you to an appropriate measured response.

CHART 14.1   Change Map

Type	Temporary Impact	Enduring Impact
Major change	Manage Deploy incident management response plan	Restart Requires a fundamental redeployment of people, plans, and practices
Minor change	Downplay Control and stay focused on priorities	Evolve Factor into ongoing team evolution

Major but Temporary Surprises

Major but temporary surprises start out either good or bad. They don't necessarily stay that way. Just as a crisis handled well can turn into a good thing, a major event handled poorly can easily turn into a serious crisis. The difference comes down to planning, implementation, and follow-through—and mostly planning. To help with these, we've included some ideas on crisis or incident management and then a little more detail on communicating in a crisis or incident in Appendix III. They are in checklist format so they are immediately actionable.

Plan in advance as much as you can by anticipating potential events and crises and having procedures in place to follow if those things happen. It is less important that you identify the actual events and crises that might come your way. The key point is that you and your organization have a response in place for unexpected events and that you periodically review the drill so you're ready to identify and react to surprises when they do hit.

When the inevitable surprise happens, pause for a moment to put in place a specific plan for that particular event or crisis using your preplanned response as a starting point. Think through the situation—your desired result and your basic approach—and map out what is going to get done by when by whom, and how you're going to communicate with all the stakeholders key to achieving your desired result.

Implement, following the basic milestone management process. The main difference is that instead of running your milestone meetings on a monthly basis, you'll likely want to make them relatively brief and run them daily if not more frequently.

Follow-through. Things have a nasty habit of getting out of control because someone takes their eyes off the ball too soon. It is hard to know when the temporary event or crisis is completely over. So, have a bias to stick with the follow through a little longer than you normally might. Then, learn from that to improve your ability to deal with the next one. There will be a next one.

Major and Enduring

Major changes that are enduring require a fundamental restart. These can be material changes in things like customer needs, collaborators' direction, competitors' strategies, or the economic, political, or social environment in which you operate. They can be internal changes such as reorganizations, acquisitions, or spin-offs.

One major and enduring change you are almost guaranteed to go through sometime is getting a new boss, or your boss getting a new boss. Take another look at the section on getting a new boss in chapter 5 and put those ideas into play immediately.

Whatever the change, if it's major and enduring, hit a restart button. Go right back to the beginning, do a full situation analysis, identify the key stakeholders, look at your message again, restart your communication campaign, and get your people, plans, and practices realigned around the new purpose. Remember, the fittest adapt best.

Don't Forget Your Communication Campaign

One of the pillars of successful leadership is an ongoing communication campaign. It needs to evolve to capitalize on changing circumstances as well. With minor changes, your message may remain the same. However, if the change is major, your message, and touch points must be adjusted to match the new reality. In some cases, the change may be significant enough to warrant a completely new communication campaign. Either way, make sure you are controlling your own message and how it is communicated.

Finis origine pendet (the end depends on the beginning)—so says the Latin poet Manilius. In a transition into a new leadership role, if you do not get the beginning right, the end will be ugly. If you follow this book's framework and take advantage of its tools, you will then be leading your team to the right place, in the right way, at the right times. If you do this, you will develop trust, loyalty, and commitment—and your team will follow. By using the proven onboarding methodologies presented in this book to enhance and synchronize your people, plans, practices (P^3) framework, you will build the tactical capacity to enable and inspire others to do their absolute best together, to realize a meaningful and rewarding shared purpose that delivers better results faster than anyone thought possible.

Critical Tools for Long-Term Leadership Success

I. Leadership—Frameworks for Thinking and Acting like a Leader

II. Situational Assessment—Guidelines for Assessing the 5Cs

III. Communication—Communication Frameworks

IV. Plans—Strategic Process

V. People and Practices—Organizational and Operational Processes

The following topics are worth exploring in greater depth: leadership, situational assessment, communication, strategy, and processes. Appendixes I through V focus on these subjects but are not intended to be exhaustive or definitive. They are designed to refresh and energize your thinking about these basic building blocks of management as you set about your 100-Day Action Plan. As we like to say to our clients: "You probably already know most, if not everything here. All we're doing is reminding you of some simple, basic principles that will help you be as effective as you can be."

Leadership

P art I of our book is called "Create Your New Leadership Role." We've broken down the components of communicating and creating leadership into a set of basic elements. Use these as a checklist to make sure you are consistently creating your own leadership potential.

1. *Listen first.* Good leaders are good connectors. They listen and read situations effectively. Many new leaders land their new role on the strength of other more narrowly defined skills or accomplishments and may have neither the natural tendency nor the opportunity to develop effective connecting skills.

    Our position on this is adamant: you must cultivate listening skills and behavior, no matter where on the spectrum you fall naturally. As with most skills, you first recognize it as something you need to develop long-term, and then you begin to practice it tactically. We recommend that you develop an ingrained habit of listening first. And even before you listen, read first. Body language, facial expressions, tone of voice—all these communicate long before words are exchanged. Remind yourself to listen and read as you go into meetings, conversations, and the like. And then review to see what key piece of knowledge allowed you to achieve the effectiveness you desired.

2. *Talk in order to listen and connect better.* Experienced communicators will talk in order to listen. They use a "Socratic" process, asking questions, or proposing possible ideas that create an environment in which key information or shifts in perspective will emerge. Connecting with the other person's likely point of view is the critical technique. This is especially important and

effective in tense or potentially conflictual situations: "Okay, let me see if I hear correctly what you are saying." "Let me take a shot at capturing your position in my own terms. Let me know if I get this wrong." The simple gesture of signaling that you want to work with that person to achieve an understanding brings down antagonism or opposition while inducing cooperation and increasing trust.

People exercise leadership by speaking deftly with a goal of connecting and helping shape the common view.

3. *Imagine the leaders' or key stakeholders' perspective.* To condition the path toward leadership, you need to see things from the leaders' broader perspective. Work to understand, as well as possible, the team's or the organization's goals and objectives. These may be explicit, or they may not (yet!) be. Actively frame your own work and the topics and issues that come up from that point of view. Leaders work to get the team to see, understand, and commit to the mission, vision, goals, strategies, and values of the group. Unappointed leaders can help move the group in this direction, and this is effort that is never lost on the leader whose responsibility it is to make this happen. By connecting to the fundamental goals of the group, you are helping your leaders and key stakeholders accomplish what they want.

4. *Identify potential areas for leadership.* If you understand the group's and your leadership goals, you will find ample opportunities to help move things along in those directions. We encourage you also to remember that your actions communicate messages far beyond the surface. Take on more responsibility than asked. Help keep a colleague from going down a wrong path. In each case, take a good measure of the opportunity in terms of what you can do, how it will shape your colleagues', subordinates', and superiors' perspective of you in the short-term, whether there are risks involved, and how this can build their positive perceptions of you as a leader long-term.

5. *Lead through:*
   - *Work:* Work is about work. If you can't do the work you're supposed to be doing, it's going to be difficult to get to where you want to be. Do good work. But don't work on stuff or in ways that don't matter to the people with whom you work.

Identify the organization's values—and in particular the leadership's values—in relationship to work and be absolutely certain that you are in sync with those values. Find the path and the structure around which the culture views basic work and make sure your career path is in alignment with it.

- *Insight:* Better than sheer work is insight. Leadership is often granted to those who show real insight. There are many ways to show insight in ways that are important to the organization. It can come from the core product or service of the organization. It can come from an insight into the core customer base, or the organizational structure, or . . . well, almost any important aspect of the business. Teams constantly need insight into helping themselves get past their challenges and to perform well. You will have opportunities on a daily basis to help frame and solve problems for your colleagues in ways that will create the leadership effect.

- *Reliability:* Reliability is a key feature for those who are promoted to leadership. But it comes in many forms and it's important to know which are likely to be important to the leadership and to the company as a whole. Shrewd leadership builders know how to shoulder a seemingly annoying or unpleasant responsibility simply to communicate that they are reliable in this way. The message should be clear; you are able and willing and can be relied on when it matters.

- *Judgment:* Senior leadership usually uses this word in making important decisions about important promotions and opportunities. Does this person have good judgment? Or, she's perfect, she has consistently shown terrific judgment, even in tough situations. Is this what would be said about you? Why? Why not? Once again, it's important to know the culture and values of the organization. Good judgment might be perceived differently in a small start-up than in a highly structured and conservative organization. The important part of judgment is knowing the framework with which the organization values decision making and being thoughtful about how any given situation might fit in with that framework. All in all, being thoughtful about implications is the hallmark of good judgment. A calculated but big risk may well be considered excellent judgment in some organizations, even if it fails. But that risk should have been given serious thought before being made.

The word *judgment* often connects to relations with people. And this brings us back to the early steps of this process— listening, connecting, understanding—as well as knowing the goals and values of the organization. Leaders lead people and have to make decisions and take actions with and about people. Even if you are not formally managing people, you are invariably involved in helping assess people and their work. Good judgment manifests itself in these informal ways long before anybody might ask you to be a manager.

- *Energy:* People underestimate the importance of energy for leadership or for the health and success of a team or organization. The leadership is often directly tied into the energy effects a person produces. Some tips:

  1. Energize the group by talking up targets and goals.
  2. Never spare kudos to individuals—praise everything good.
  3. Be sparing of negative comments and pep talks, but use them as appropriate.
  4. Make sure the team finds ways to celebrate successes.
  5. Be attuned to negative moods in individuals or the group and seek to find what may be causing it.
  6. Watch your own moods and find ways to turn them positive.

- *Humor:* Look for ways to use humor to bond and energize the group. A common failing among leaders or potential leaders is a lack of self-deprecating humor. The opposite—humor at others' expense—is counterproductive. If that's the way your humor runs, learn to redirect it. It will just get you in trouble. Since we're talking about getting in trouble, be careful about the humor that comes out in more informal situations, especially if drinking is involved. Steer yourself out of trouble, and help your colleagues do the same.

- *Conflict:* Conflicts can freeze teams and cripple organizations. Therefore, they are opportunities for leadership. Avoid needless conflict yourself. A tendency to get into and mishandle conflict can absolutely collapse your career.

Groups almost inescapably have internal conflict. A key sign of a leader is someone who can help the group handle its conflicts better. Avoid taking sides, and look for paths out of the conflict. If you've been doing your homework—listening, connecting, and understanding both the individuals and the group's goals (by the way, humor is key here)—you will have the tools to help shift the group to a better place. And the group will appreciate and look to you for leadership as a result.

- *Inspiration:* Maybe this should have come first, but last works, too. Successful leaders tend to know how to tap into concepts and language that inspire people. Values and goals inspire people. Personal passion and commitment inspire people. Family, humanity, and personal connection inspire people. Inspiration is the difference between a team that comes in, does its work, and checks out versus one where people derive significant personal satisfaction from their work and the success of their team. The building blocks are the individual relationships you have with your colleagues. You can begin to activate inspiration long before you're in a position to set goals for a team and challenge team members to successes.

6. *Carpe diem.* We hope that this has helped put you in a state of mind where you see that, yes, you can build a leadership effect through a methodical and proactive approach to your colleagues and your workplace. Sooner or later, and if you've been effective in the preceding ways, sooner rather than later, a key leadership opportunity will emerge. You will need to act decisively. If you've been thinking about this, you are likely to recognize the opportunity. Think in advance about how you respond to situations where there is a lot at stake.

   Many of us behave differently than we usually do, often to our detriment. Impulsive or panicky behavior is typical. A deep-seated fight-or-flight response can kick in. Generally speaking, neither one is best suited for the occasion. That is not to say that a calculated strategy of fighting or fleeing might not be the best response. Just that it should be thought through.

In any case, consider carefully how you typically respond and what you can do to make sure you respond the way you want to. Answering certain questions can help you get ready in advance. Are you prepared for a change in responsibilities? Are you willing to undertake a certain amount of risk or discomfort? How can you give yourself time for composure? Finally, how can you back away from your own volatile feelings to the core elements of leadership—listening, connecting, understanding, and goal setting—and make sure you are communicating these things even in the midst of this situation?

If you've prepared your career plan and worked through the leadership elements we've discussed here, you should be in excellent shape. Remember Steps Four and Five of the Five-Step Career Plan—Options and Choice. You have done the work for this, just spend some time considering that the opportunity may jump out suddenly, and you need to be ready to act.

Situational Assessment

The fundamental purpose of this tool is to assess what's going on with your customers, collaborators, capabilities, competitors, and conditions (5Cs) and put that into a SWOT analysis so you can figure out your key leverage points and business issues.

The 5Cs

- *Customers:* First line, customer chain, end users, influencers
- *Collaborators:* Suppliers, allies, government/community leaders
- *Capabilities:* Human, operational, financial, technical, key assets
- *Competitors:* Direct, indirect, potential
- *Conditions:* Social/demographic, political/government/regulatory, economic, market

Customers include the people your business sells to—direct customers who actually give you money. It also includes their customers, their customers' customers, and so on down the line. Eventually, there are end users or consumers of whatever the output of that chain is. Finally, there are the people who influence your various customers' purchase decisions. Take all of these into account.

Federal Express sells overnight delivery services to corporate purchasing departments that contract those services on behalf of business managers. But the real decision makers are those managers' administrative assistants. So, Federal Express targets its marketing efforts not at the people who write the checks, not at the managers, but at the core influencers. They aim advertising and media at those influencers and have their drivers pick the packages up from the administrative assistants personally instead of going through an impersonal mailroom.

Collaborators include your suppliers, business allies, and people delivering complementary products and services. What links all these groups together is that they will do better if you do better, so it's in their best interest, whether they know it or not, to help you succeed. Think Microsoft and Intel. Think hot dogs and mustard.

Just as these relationships are two-way, so must be your analysis. You need to understand the interdependencies and reciprocal commitments. Whenever these dependencies and commitments are out of balance, the nature of the relationships will inevitably change.

Capabilities are those abilities that can help you deliver a differentiated, better product or service to your customers. These include everything from access to materials and capital to plants and equipment to people to patents. Pay particular attention to people, plans, and practices.

Competitors are anyone that your customers could give their money or attention to instead of to you. Without restating everything everyone has ever said about marketing myopia, it is important to take a wide view of potential competitors. Amtrak's real competitors are other forms of transportation like automobiles and airplanes. The competition for consumer dollars may be as varied as a child's college education versus a Disney World vacation. In analyzing these competitors, it is important to think through their objectives and strategies as well as strengths and weaknesses to give you the best possible chance to predict what they will really do.

Conditions are a catchall for everything going on in the environment in which you do business. At a minimum, look at social and political, demographic, and economic trends. Also, think through the implications of those trends on your new organization's likelihood of success over the short-, mid-, and long-term.

5Cs Analysis*

1. Customers (First Line, Customer Chain, End Users, Influencers)
Needs, hopes, preference, commitment, strategies, price/value perspective by segment

First Line/Direct Customers:
Universe of opportunity—total market, volume by segment
Current situation—volume by customer; profit by customer
Customer Chain:
Customers' customers—total market, volume by segment
Current customers' strategies, volume, and profitability by segment
*End Users:*Preference, consumption, usage, loyalty, and price value data and perceptions for our products and competitors' products
Influencers:
Key influencers of customer and end user purchase and usage decisions

2. Collaborators (Suppliers, Business Allies, Complementors, Government/ community Leaders)
Strategies, profit/value models for external and internal stakeholders (up, across, down)

3. Capabilities
Human (includes style and quality of management; strategy dissemination; culture: values, norms, focus, discipline, innovation, teamwork, execution, urgency, politics)
Operational (includes integrity of business processes, effectiveness of organization structure, links between measures and rewards and corporate governance)
Financial (includes capital and asset utilization and investor management)
Technical (includes core processes, IT systems, supporting skills)
Key assets (includes brands and intellectual property)

(continued)

---

4. Competitors (Direct, Indirect, Potential)
Strategies, profit/value models, profit pools by segment, source of pride

5. Conditions
Social/demographic—trends
Political/government/regulatory—trends
Economic—macro and micro—trends
Market definition, inflows, outflows, substitutes, etc.—trends

PULLING IT TOGETHER:

SWOT analysis and thinking about:
Sources, drivers, and hinderers of revenue and value
Current strategy/resource deployment: Coherent? Adequate? De facto strategy?
Insights and scenarios (To set up: What?/So what?/Now what?)

SWOT

A SWOT (internal **S**trengths and **W**eaknesses versus external **O**pportunities and **T**hreats) analysis is a good way to summarize this and lay out the current reality (see Tool A2.2).

Key leverage points are the internal strengths that can be brought to bear to take advantage of external opportunities. These are the corridors of ways to win. For example, if you have a strong beverage distribution system and the public water supply is contaminated, you could leverage your system to deliver safe bottled water to people.

Business issues are the areas of internal weakness that are particularly vulnerable to external threats. Fixing these are ways to avoid losing. If you have only marginally acceptable safety standards in your plants and there is pending legislation to increase legal safety standards well beyond those that you currently meet, that is a potential issue.

Finally, the sustainable competitive advantage is most likely one of the key leverage points that can be sustained in the face of business issues.

Use a SWOT to prompt your thinking in three areas:

1. Sources, drivers, and hinderers of revenue and value
2. Current strategy/resource deployment: Coherent? Adequate? De facto strategy?
3. Insights and scenarios (to set up: What?/So what?/Now what?)

Sources, Drivers, and Hinderers of Revenue and Value

- *Sources* of revenue and value. For example, energy is coming from the dam.

- *Drivers* of how to turn that potential into reality? Turbines create energy.

- *Hinderers* keeping us from doing better? For example, turbines' capacity of 1,000,000 gallons a day.

Understanding the sources, drivers, and hinderers gives you more information to drive insights.

Current Strategy/Resource Deployment: Coherent? Adequate? De Facto Strategy?

- *Coherent?* Are your resources deployed so each is moving you in the *same direction?* It is scary how many times one part of the organization is doing things to strengthen one area while another part of the same organization is doing things that weaken the same area. For example, marketing tells people that brand X should be compared with products in category A, and then sales puts the brand on the shelf next to products in category B.
- *Adequate?* Do you have enough resources deployed to achieve your objectives?
- *De facto strategy?* How does what you're actually doing match your stated strategy? For example, discount pricing in the market doesn't match a stated strategy of premium positioning.

Insights and Scenarios (to Set Up: What?/So What?/Now What?)

The SWOT gives you data to start thinking about scenarios and opportunities. "What?/So what?/Now what?" is a thinking model I've used for decades:

- *What?* Gets at the facts or data. These are things you see and know. No judgment or bias is involved, and anyone looking at the facts or data would see the same thing: the turbines can handle 1,000,000 gallons of water a day.
- *So what?* Gets at what you think about the facts or data. For these conclusions, you add in your knowledge and judgment: the 1,000,000-gallon per day capacity of the turbines is a hinderer. The moment I labeled this a "hinderer," I drew a conclusion.
- *Now what?* Gets at actions to be taken given these conclusions: add more turbines.

SWOT Form*

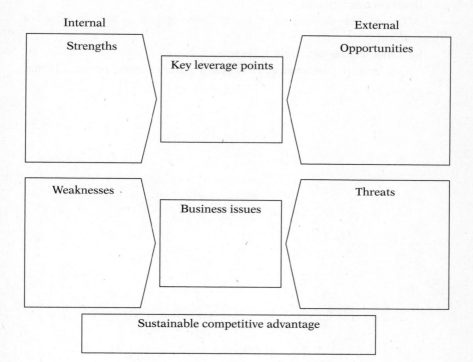

Strengths	Internal to organization—things we do better
Weaknesses	Internal to organization—things we do worse
Opportunities	External to organization—things to capitalize on
Threats	External to organization—things to worry about

(continued)

Key Leverage Points

Opportunities we can leverage our strengths against (where to play to win)

Business Implications

Threats our weaknesses make us vulnerable to (where to play not to lose)

Sustainable Competitive Advantages

Key leverage points that can be sustained over extended periods of time

Communication

Much of what we have to say about communication you probably know already. But you may not know how to activate this knowledge into an effective overall communication plan and a concrete communication campaign in your first 100 Days and beyond. You also may not realize just how important some of the more oblique aspects of communication really are. As you go through our general principles, consider them, and test them, you will be on a path to becoming a great communicator as well as to having a successful first 100 Days.

Words Are Only a Small Part of the Game

It's not about the words. This may seem paradoxical or just wrong to you. Words are important. However, communication takes place on many nonverbal levels, and it's essential to develop skills in reading and using these nonverbal modes.

Context or Frame

Great communicators know how to choose or create the right context or frame for their messages. This can be choosing a large group versus a one-on-one situation, a casual circumstance versus a formal one. Or it can be the simple act of framing a message or a conversation: "I think this makes the most sense if you look at it in the context of optimizing resources." Or alternatively, it can be setting the mood for a talk, conversation, or event by using humor, empathy, or other connective tactics. Large and small, literal circumstance or verbal context, we communicate in a context that is either chosen or created by us, or simply given.

The more you develop an awareness of how context or frame conditions the meaning and the reception of messages, the more effective your communications will be. You can start by observing carefully how context and frame are affecting communications in general, then noting carefully how masterful communicators manage it, and then by developing the skill.

Timing

This is an extension of context or frame, specific to time and timing. Timing is everything for jokes, and for marriage proposals, and for every important communication.

Develop a keen awareness of how good or off your own timing is. Watch others who seem to get this right. Think carefully about the bigger picture—if I bring this up at this point, will it be more or less effective than holding it until x, y, or z happens? What if I say this first? Or earlier than expected?

A big part of timing is what others are expecting, what "is expected." Good communicators are very much in touch with expectations and play with and against those expectations to increase effect. It goes without saying that sometimes, not saying anything or not saying what is expected can be just as effective as anything you might say.

Style

Leaders tend to have, or develop, a different communication style from those who are not leaders. There are many styles of leadership, but the style is an important part of the message. Style can be completely nonverbal—posture, tone, and timbre of voice, eye contact, smiling or other facial expressions, and proximity to others. Verbal delivery is also a matter of style.

For the vast majority of us, this style is almost entirely unconscious. It is just "who we are." Or, and this is important, it is a reflection of our mood or state of mind, or a reflection of the people you happen to be with. If your goal is to control your message and assure its effectiveness, you want this to be a more conscious and controlled feature. This is not the same, by the way, as having a highly self-conscious style. A winning style is often the opposite—natural and authentic.

These people know that this is how they come across and how they are. You can be aware and not stiffly self-conscious. Become aware of how style affects communication in yourself and others, and cultivate a style that suits your personality and your goals best.

Body Language (Especially Eye Contact)

This is subset of style, but worth underlining. Good communicators read body language very well and are good at using body language to good effect. To communicate, you need to connect. And a sense of connection or the lack of it is very strongly communicated and created through body language.

In face-to-face interaction, eye contact is the fundamental element. Strong, frank, and open eye contact is the sign of an engaged listener and speaker. Observe yourself. If you find your eyes sliding away from all steady contact, you have serious work to do.

Body language is highly imitative, almost contagious. Part of context and timing is recognizing when and if the body language is propitious for your communication goal. Or knowing how to create the atmosphere of body language that you want or need. We have seen many leaders highly hampered in their ability to lead effectively because of a sense of separation or disconnectedness that is readable in their own body language and those of their colleagues, superiors, and subordinates. We've also seen some remarkable turnarounds as they adopt a new sensitivity and approach.

A key area of opportunity is the whole realm of unofficial interaction. You need to learn how to use such interactions to create a sense of connection and engagement, and then how to transition to the more official or formal elements of the communication campaign.

Actions

Words and speech are actions, obviously. But a communication plan is greatly enhanced by an awareness of how certain kinds of actions (which can mean not doing something) shape, affect, support, or simply make the communication. A big area of nonverbal action revolves around showing up. Being present. To meetings. On time, early or late. In somebody's office. At casual events. Or following up on a promise.

Or making (or not making) an important decision. In the world of the first 100 Days, decisions about organizational structure are probably the most loaded of all. Here, timing is everything. From a communication point of view, it is important to think through what will be most effective—let the action speak for itself? Support it? Explain it? Prepare it? Follow up on it?

Inaction and Silence

We have already called attention to this, but it's so important it merits special attention. It can be easy to get caught in a kind of frenzy of action and communication. But if we think back to the basics of leadership and the idea that the leader is measured, thoughtful, and reliable, the lack of action or speaking can actually communicate this most effectively. It also suggests (and can help you achieve) an approach that is thought out and not simply reactive. This is all part of style, and we all have our own. But it is important to know the tools of communication if you want to use them effectively.

Rhythm and Repetition

We talked about speaking style. But there is also frequency and duration. We have seen huge benefits occur almost immediately when people who tend to talk too much, or go on too long, learn how to interrupt themselves, thus creating more space for the people they interact with. (Along with eye contact, this can be extremely effective.) Conversely, we have seen sharply positive reversals happen when people who tend to speak too little, or too formally, learn how to mix it up and volunteer more often.

Going back to the overall goal of a communication campaign, repetition is the key to success. The message has to be clear, short, and continually repeated.

Visuals

Many people simply respond better to visual information, either literally in printed form or on a computer screen, or in the form of visual imagery and analogies.

Second- and Third-Hand Channels

It is remarkable how effective second- and third-hand channels of communication are. Many highly self-directed people, natural choices for leaders, are particularly weak in their awareness of, appreciation for, or ability to use these channels. Great communicators know how to energize these channels to enhance the impact of their communication campaign as well as to measure its effectiveness.

Words

Let's return now to words—in fact, we urge you to see words and nonverbal communication as part of a continuum. We emphasize the nonverbal aspect since this is a skill set many new leaders (and even established ones) need to develop.

Less Is More

People complain about sound bites, but the fact is, the method works. And it is nothing new. The great classical orators—from Cicero to Abraham Lincoln—knew a thing or two about sound biting. Brief sentences have more impact. Succinct explanations are understood better. Big concepts are remembered longer.

Too much information stifles attention, bewilders the understanding, and saps the will. Keep it short. Keep it simple.

Once Is Never Enough

To get your message across, you need to repeat it. A lot. Don't underestimate the importance and value of repeating, repeating, repeating. Mix it up. But drill it home.

Test for Reception, Understanding, Agreement, Enthusiasm

People often speak and write to each other without any real communication taking place. The way to achieve effective communication is to test for effectiveness. This can be done directly—"What do you think? Does what I'm saying make sense to you?" or more indirectly, "I'd love to hear other people's thoughts on this topic. Maybe I'm missing something really important here that hasn't yet been brought out." Nonverbal cues can guide you to how directly you should test and whether you need to change course.

Emotion Communicates

Much our education and professional work is based on argument, logic, and analysis. In certain environments, that really is the only way to communicate. But in the larger, fuzzier world of teamwork and team leadership, it's a huge mistake to rely on these hard-edged modes of communication. Communicate and connect through emotion. Acknowledge and show awareness of emotion—positive ones, negative ones. Connect your core message to emotional registers you know are important for you, your team, and your organization.

Framers Win

Communication is largely about framing. It is said that "facts speak for themselves." But the truth is that people who help frame the facts are the most effective in communicating.

Sincerity and Passion Conquer All

It's important to begin and end with this point. Sincerity and passion are the core elements of effective communication and leadership. People do not follow insincere leaders, and they don't really listen to them. They also don't follow diffident leaders. This is why we have everyone use their core values as the foundation for their career plan. That foundation in turn drives the momentum for success in the 100-Day Plan. Stay in touch with your own values and your own passion, and much of the rest will simply follow suit.

As you craft your communication campaign you will also be shaping your culture with the roll out of that campaign. Tool A3.1 provides a good framework for thinking about driving cultural change. Keep in mind that there will always be people aiding or hindering your progress toward your desired cultural change.

Downloadable TOOL A3.1
Culture Change Management*

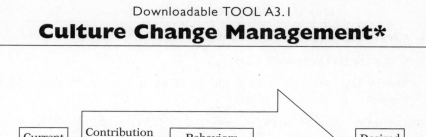

1. **Identify the New Desired Culture You Are Trying to Create.**

_____
_____
_____
_____

2. **Evaluate Current Culture: Behaviors, Attitudes, Contributors, Detractors.**

_____
_____
_____
_____

3. **Detail What Changes Need to Be Made to Move From Current to New.**
   Consider the impact of shifts
   Key considerations/changes

_____
_____
_____
_____

(continued)

4. **Create Communication and Change Plan.**

    Change map of key stakeholders

    Identify key individuals' roles in change (block it, watch it, help it, make it happen)

    Determine effective ways to move stakeholders to appropriate levels of support

    Develop and implement a detailed communication plan

    _____

    _____

    _____

    _____

5. **Test Progress at Checkpoints along the Way.**

Downloadable TOOL A3.2

Communication Planning*

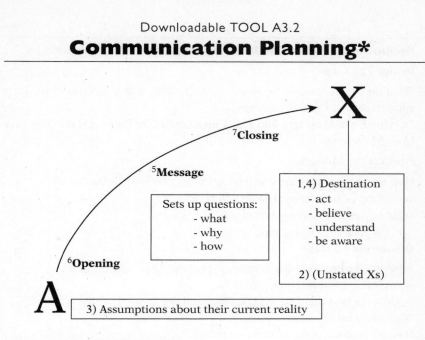

X

[7]**Closing**

[5]**Message**

Sets up questions:
- what
- why
- how

1,4) Destination
- act
- believe
- understand
- be aware

2) (Unstated Xs)

[6]**Opening**

A

3) Assumptions about their current reality

1. **Identify Your Destination.**** ,

   What is the desired reaction and behavior you want from your audience/constituents?

   What specifically do you want/not want them to understand, believe, say about you, or do?

2. **Be Explicit about Unstated Xs.**

   What do you want listeners to think about you?

3. **Assess Current Reality.**

   What does your audience/constituency currently understand, believe, say about you? Why?

   Develop a risk management plan including potential obstacles, negative rumors, sabotage, legal requirements, unintended consequences, and scenarios.

   (continued)

**Much of this is based on work by Sandy Linver and her company Speakeasy, also laid out in her book *Speak and Get Results,* New York: Simon & Schuster, 1994.

4. **Reevaluate Destination in Light of Assumptions about Audience.**

5. **Bridge The Gap.**

   What do people need to be aware of, understand, and believe to move from current reality to your destination?

6. **Develop Core Messages and Key Communication Points (Maximum Five Core Messages).**

7. **Package the Message.**

   How should core messages be packaged for optimum effectiveness?
   What kind of supporting data do you need?
   What is your key opening message?
   What is your key closing message?

8. **Deliver the Message.**

   What are the best vehicles to reach your audience or constituents?
   What is the optimum combination?
   What is the best timing to release the message?
   Who and what influences whom?
   How do you best plant the follow-up seeds?

Downloadable TOOL A3.3
Press Interviews*

The key point is to take control of the interview. Time is on your side if you stay focused on what you want to communicate and you control the dialogue, just as it's on others' sides if they control the dialogue.

Prepare
Objective—What do you want out of the interaction?

Anticipate questions—Know interviewer, audience, and their interest factors (competition, conflict, controversy, consequences, familiar person, heartstrings, humor, problem, progress, success, unknown, unusual, wants/needs).

Approach—How do you choose to go about achieving the objective? There are always different ways to get there. Consider them and choose one. This will lead to:

> Key communication points—Key points you want to drive home (three maximum). This will allow you to do more than just answer questions (questions are merely cues for your key points). These points need:

> Support—Facts, personal experience, contrast/compare, analogy, expert opinion, analysis, definition, statistics, and examples.

Deliver
Be clear, concise, complete (do one thing well), constructive, credible, controversial, captivating, correct (must correct significant errors on the part of interviewers or press).

Be yourself, liked, prepared, enthusiastic, specific, correct, anecdotal, listen, bridge, cool.

Follow-Through
Deliver on commitments.

Think through what worked particularly well and less well to improve for the future.

Downloadable TOOL A3.4
Crisis Management Checklist*

In almost any crisis management situation, you should prepare, understand, plan, implement, and revise or prepare:

Prepare
Have an incident/crisis management team and process in place and ready to go in advance.

Understand
Pause for a moment to figure out what you know and think:

What do we know for a fact?

What do we not know, but need to know?

What do we think/conclude is going on?

What do we predict may happen (scenarios)?

What are the potential issues and risks?

Do a quick SWOT analysis (strengths, weaknesses, opportunities, threats):
What are our assets?

Gaps?

Situational things we can take advantage of?

Risks?

Plan
What do we want to happen (under the different scenarios)?
What do we need to do to make that happen (under different scenarios)?
Immediate actions to fix problem
Long-term actions to prevent recurrence

What will we communicate to all our constituents (consumers, customers, management, employees, media, health authorities)?
In what order will we communicate to them?

Will our communication be proactive or reactive?

Identify single crisis manager.

Identify single spokesperson.

Clarify exactly what you are doing with what resources and when you are doing it.

Implement

Move quickly and decisively to contain and control incident:

Isolate the situation (contain; prevent spreading; limit entry to prevent extraneous people and factors from interfering and complicating the situation).

Deal with injury.

Stabilize the situation: stop momentum (Take no actions that exacerbate the situation or create new problems such as placing blame, making inflammatory comments, or ignoring the opinions and recommendations of others).

Provide frequent updates as information gaps are filled:

Assemble and evaluate accuracy of available information.

Notify and update community contacts (police, fire, etc.).

Set up operations and communications centers.

Delegate responsibility for functional support/response teams and communication.

Monitor and track the situation progress and response and adjust as needed:

Ensure stability.

Reconfirm accuracy of information and keep communication channels open.

Offer trauma counseling.

Continue to liaison with authorities.

Keep all promises made.

Overcommunicate across team every step of the way.

When the crisis/incident is over, thank authorities and contributors.

Revise or Prepare

General debrief:

When were we aware of the incident/event?

What signals were recognized, not recognized?

When did we first sense a problem?

When did it become a crisis?

What caused the crisis?

What was considered in prior vulnerability inventory?

(continued)

Did we accurately assess impact of problem?

Have we ever rehearsed for this?

Debrief planning:

Did we plan effectively? What improvements can we make?

Were the necessary resources (medical, legal, PR, technical, management, or an effective notification system) available?

How effective was the written plan?

Were our people knowledgeable about their roles and others' roles?

Was there any undue confusion or conflict?

Were sufficient personnel available with the right mix?

Did we have adequate equipment, facilities, and resources? Was anything inadequate, in need of change or enhancement?

How current was the information?

Debrief success or failure:

How quickly did we bring the crisis under control?

How well did we work with government agencies?

How well did we communicate with key audiences?

What was the public's view of our actions?

What was the view of other audiences?

What is our own view of our actions? Did we meet our own objectives?

How well did we preserve our credibility?

What steps can we take now to ensure continued productive company operations?

Lessons/trends to share with others: What did we do particularly well that should be continued and cascaded? What needs to be improved?

Modify policies and practices as appropriate.

Downloadable TOOL A3.5
Crisis Communication Checklist*

Communication Preparation

Anticipate questions.

Know each audience and its interest factors (competition, conflict, controversy, consequences, familiar person, heartstrings, humor, problem, progress, success, unknown, unusual, wants/needs). Your SWOT analysis as recommended previously will answer some of these questions.

Communication Approach

There are usually many ways to communicate and many possible messages to convey. There are many choices and often they need to be made quickly. Before going forward, you'll need to decide:

What method of communication is the best to achieve our objective?

_____

_____

What **key messages** (no more than three) do we want to drive?

_____

_____

Make everyone in a position of communication aware of the key messages. Insist that they focus on them. Consider questions as merely cues to drive home the key messages. Time and control remain on your side if you focus on controlling the dialogue by concentrating on the key messages. If you move beyond the key messages, the other side will assume control of the dialogue, which is usually not advantageous to your communication objectives.

(continued)

How can you **support** your key points? You can find support in facts, personal experience, contrasts, comparisons, analogies, expert opinion, analysis, definition, statistics, and examples.

Once you have your method of communication, your key communication points, and your support, you can then move into implementation.

Communication Implementation
Show concern (especially if there's a crisis).
Communicate quickly (no indecision).
Communicate credibly (tell the truth, release only confirmed facts, correct significant errors and counteract negatives, stay calm).
Communicate thoroughly (proactively release updates).
After the incident, communication does not stop. Be prepared to **revise and prepare** for the next communication attempt. In some crises of great magnitude or high interest, several cycles of communication may stretch over long periods. If there is just one communication event, most likely others will follow at some point in the future. Therefore, this last and final step is essential.

Plans—Strategic Process

The strategic process is the first of the three critical ongoing processes required to run a business: the other two are operational process and organizational process. This is a two-part appendix: There is a discussion of mission, vision, and values; it is followed by an examination of an effective strategic planning process.

Mission

Simply put, a mission statement informs the organization how to spend its time. However, mission statements are often so complex and convoluted that they do not have meaning to anyone. The best mission statements are concise, clear, and motivating. They leave no question as to the "higher good" or the "ultimate focus" of the organization:

> Provide relief *to victims of disasters and help people prevent, prepare for, and respond to emergencies.*
> —American Red Cross

> Preserve and improve *human life*
> —Merck

> *To* explore *new worlds, discover new civilizations; seek out new life forms, and to boldly go where no one has gone before.*
> —Starship Enterprise

Vision

A good vision is an appealing picture of future success, showing what the company will be like when the mission is accomplished. Some examples of clear and inspiring visions:

> *The world's premier engineering organization. Trained and ready to provide support any time, any place.*
> —*U.S. Army Corps of Engineers*

> *Create a world-renowned, yet personable, showcase of maverick films, filmmakers and the technology that enables creativity.*
> —*Cinequest*

> *A world in which every child, every where, has equal access to life-saving vaccines*
> —*The Vaccine Fund*

Objectives are the broadly defined, qualitative performance requirements of the business such as achieving market leadership or dominating a category. Objectives should be closely related to the company's vision. If the vision is "A world in which every child, every where, has equal access to life-saving vaccines," the objectives might be: (1) creation of vaccines, (2) manufacture of vaccines, (3) awareness of vaccines, (4) funding for vaccines, and (5) distribution of vaccines.

Goals flow out of objectives. Goals need to be SMART (Specific, Measurable, Attainable, Relevant, and Time bound) and follow from objectives. If the main objective is creation of vaccines, the goal could be to develop three market-ready vaccines by June 30.

Strategy is about the creation and allocation of resources to the right place in the right way at the right time over time. By corollary, there is a wrong place, a wrong way, and a wrong time. So, strategy boils down to selecting which options to pursue and which options not to pursue. As Michael Porter puts it, "Strategy is choosing what not to do."[1] The tough choices come in choosing not to pursue an option that is a good idea—but for someone else or at a different time. A simple way to drive strategic choices is by asking two questions: Where are we going to play? How are we going to win? Simple and focused.

---

[1] Michael Porter—*Harvard Lecture.*

Values are the beliefs and moral principles that guide actions and decisions—these are things that a team cannot walk away from to pursue its mission and vision. Value-driven teams do *not* believe the end justifies the means. Values are important to them because they guide both individuals and teams on a day-to-day basis.

Strategic Planning

Strategic planning is about generating and selecting options. It is how the gaps between objectives and current reality are delineated and resources are re-assessed to generate practical, immediate options for building the momentum that will close those gaps. For us, strategic planning is tightly correlated to practical goals and concrete benchmarks for success. It is also bound up with building and executing the Burning Imperative that begins the program.

Development Process

You can think about strategy development in two steps:

1. Creating a set of strategic options
2. Choosing which ones to pursue

In the end, you are trying to come up with the best strategy to get you from your *current reality* to your *destination*. Unless you are already there, there is a *gap* between where you are and where you want to be. It is also likely that there are some *barriers* keeping that gap in place. The strategy will guide your *actions* in bridging that gap. This is depicted in Figure A4.1.

We have drawn A4.1 as a two-dimensional figure to show that there are different possible routes to get from the current reality to the destination. Of course, it is really a multidimensional world with multiple different routes. But, sticking with the figure we've drawn, thinking in terms of a couple of dimensions helps create different options.

If you were trying to increase sales, one dimension might be sales to existing customers. Another might be the number of customers. You can increase total sales by moving along either dimension. Adding new customers might involve recruiting sales "hunters" particularly adept at wooing new customers to overcome the barrier of not being able to contact enough customers. Increasing sales to existing customers

FIGURE A4.1 Destination Planning

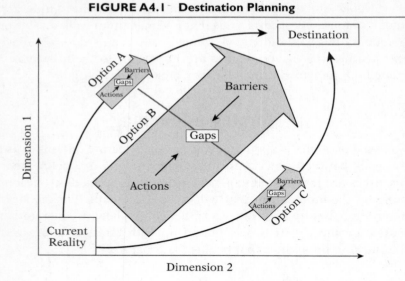

might involve recruiting client service "farmers" particularly adept at building deep relationships to overcome the barrier of not knowing enough about your current customers.

Basic Steps

Here is a basic flow for strategic planning. It is a complete, robust planning process. Of course, different organizations will modify it to meet their needs. Some separate long-term planning from annual planning. Some use different processes for different organizations. We are not suggesting that this is the only way to do this. But it is a good way.

1. Set the aspirational *destination*.
2. Assess the facts of the *current reality* and develop future *scenarios*.
3. Identify *options* to bridge gaps between reality and aspiration:
   - Peer and management *input* to enhance scenarios and options.
4. *Evaluate* options under different scenarios:
   - Peer and management *involvement* to understand and improve valuation assumptions.
   - Management *agreement* on which options to pursue.
5. Develop detailed business *plans*.
6. *Act, measure, adjust, and repeat.*

Step 1: Set the Aspirational Destination
Strategic planning begins with the aspirational long-term *destination*, which should look a lot like the vision. It is important for this step to come before looking at the current reality. Starting with the current reality forces your team to build *from* the current existence, which results in a strategy that often leads to a place short of the aspirational destination. Starting with the end in mind, the aspirational destination allows the team to build a clear and direct path *toward* the aspiration.

Step 2: Assess the Facts of the Current Reality and Develop Future Scenarios
The next step is to analyze the current reality. This involves reviewing, once again, the 5Cs: *customers, collaborators, capabilities, competitors,* and *conditions* as well as performing a SWOT (Strengths, Weaknesses, Opportunities, Threats) analysis.

Scenarios

Scenarios involve potential changes to the external world. They are generally outside the control of the organization. Given this, the organization cannot choose which one will happen, but it can lay out expected probabilities for each scenario happening. This is useful in terms of evaluating the expected results of different strategic options later.

One of the fundamental realities for Walt Disney in creating Walt Disney World in Florida was that he had to assemble a large tract of land that was currently in the hands of multiple landowners. He had money, but no local knowledge. The scenarios involved who found out what he was trying to do and when they found it out.

Step 3: Identify Options to Bridge Gaps between Reality and Aspiration
The basic question you should ask yourself is which strategic options might create additional value—or minimize its destruction. This is where creativity comes in as you come up with a range of options that could potentially address the issues and move the organization forward. For ideas, look hard at your key leverage points for offensive options and at your key business issues for defensive options.

This is a good time to get peer and management input into your thinking. You are trying to collect ideas. If peers or management have good ideas, you want to know about them. You are not looking for decisions yet, just input.

Some of Disney's options in Florida included buying the land himself, going through the local government and leveraging their rights of eminent domain, or buying the land behind the scenes through a third party.

Step 4: Evaluate Options under Different Scenarios
The question here is which strategic options create the most value over time, risk adjusted, under different scenarios. You'll want to evaluate options and scenarios leading to a range of forecasts based on transparent assumptions. At this point, the key stakeholders should become involved to understand and help improve the components of the valuation assumptions. Then, separately and later, you will want to get these key stakeholders involved to agree on which options to pursue.

Remember the three stakeholder points of involvement:

1. Input to enhance scenarios and options—capturing their ideas
2. Involvement to understand and improve valuation assumptions—tapping into their experience and context
3. Agreement on which options to pursue (which should fall out of the expected valuation of different options under different scenarios)

In Florida, Disney chose to engage outside companies to buy the various parcels of land, overcoming the barrier that prices would rise if people knew what he was trying to do. He chose not to try to assemble the land himself or in his own name or through the local government.

Step 5: Develop Detailed Business Plans
This is where you think through what strategic, operational, and organizational actions are needed to implement each selected option.

- *Strategic plan:* Strategic posture (shape the industry of the future, adapt to the future, reserve right to play), resource allocation, rules of engagement across critical business drivers
- *Action plan:* Actions, timetables, roles, responsibilities, linkages—for both immediate impact programs and capability enhancements

- *Multiyear resource plan:* Human, financial, operational—requirements, application, sources
- *Performance management plan:* Operating and financial performance standards, measures, and goals

Step 6: Act, Measure, Adjust, and Repeat

Smith Kline Beecham had a useful way of evaluating options. The steps they used are incorporated into Steps 2–5 above. Done right, the choice of which option to pursue falls out of the scenario/option grid. Let's stick with our increasing sales example as an oversimplified way of showing this. Recall, the basic dimensions were increasing sales to existing customers (farming) or adding new customers (hunting).

Assume three scenarios for the future of the industry:

1. *Industry consolidation:* Number of customers shrinking
2. *Industry stagnation:* Number of customers constant
3. *Industry expansion:* Number of customers increasing

To determine which of your strategic options (hunting, farming, or neither) has the highest expected value, you need to figure out what the payoff will be under each scenario and the probabilities of each happening.

Assume that hunters cost $100K each and generate $200K in a period of expansion, $50K during stagnation, and $25K during consolidation. Let's also assume that farmers cost $50K and generate $25K in a period of expansion, $40K during stagnation, and $100K during consolidation. Looking at the options of adding either 10 hunters, adding 10 farmers, or adding nothing would produce a grid like this:

Profit Change ($000)		Expansion	Stagnation	Contraction
Add 10 hunters		1,000	−500	−750
Add none		0	0	0
Add 10 farmers		−250	−100	500
	Costs	Revenue	Revenue	Revenue
New hunter	100	200	50	25
New farmer	50	25	40	100

In a time of expansion, the best option is to add hunters so they can woo new market entrants. In a time of stagnation, the best option is to do nothing. In a time of contraction, the best option is to add farmers so they can capture existing customers' increasing market shares. It is easy to choose if you know what is going to happen. But if there is uncertainty as to which scenario will play out, the action choice is driven by the expected likelihood of each scenario.

If the bias is toward expansion, you might see something like this, leading us to add hunters:

Expansion Bias

Profit Change ($000)	Expansion	Stagnation	Contraction	Expected
Add 10 hunters	1,000	−500	−750	188
Add none	0	0	0	0
Add 10 farmers	−250	−100	500	−25
Probability (%)	50	25	25	
	Costs	Revenue	Revenue	Revenue
New hunter	100	200	50	25
New farmer	50	25	40	100

Conversely, a contraction bias would look like this (adding farmers):

Contraction Bias

Profit Change ($000)	Expansion	Stagnation	Contraction	Expected
Add 10 hunters	1,000	−500	−750	−250
Add none	0	0	0	0
Add 10 farmers	−250	−100	50	163
Probability (%)	25	25	50	
	Costs	Revenue	Revenue	Revenue
New hunter	100	200	50	25
New farmer	50	25	40	100

The different probabilities lead you to different choices. If you think the likelihood of expansion is greater, the expected value of the hunter-focused option wins. If you think the likelihood of contraction is greater, you'll add farmers instead. Here we see the same scenarios, same options, same revenues and costs, but different choices. This is why it is so important to get everyone aligned around the assumptions.

Strategic Planning Summary

Strategic planning begins with the aspirational destination that is drawn from the vision and objectives from the imperative:

- Analyze the *current reality using the 5Cs approach*.
- Complete a SWOT summary.
- Create *strategy* options to guide *actions*, overcome *barriers*, and bridge *gaps*.
- Get key stakeholder input into options and assumptions.
- Get key stakeholder agreement on which strategic options to pursue.
- Develop four key business plans:
  1. Strategic plan
  2. Action plan
  3. Resource plan
  4. Performance management plan

People and Practices— Organizational and Operational Processes

An ADEPT Framework for Talent Management

ADEPT FLOW

Acquire | Develop | Encourage | Plan | Transition

Acquire   Scope roles.
Identify prospects.
Recruit and select the right people for the right roles.
Attract those people.
Onboard them so they can deliver better results faster.

Develop   Assess performance drivers.
Develop skills and knowledge for current and future roles.

Encourage   Say "please" by providing clear direction, objectives, measures, etc.
Support with the resources and time require for success.
Say "thank you" with recognition and rewards.

Plan   Monitor peoples' performance over time.
Assess their situation and potential.
Plan career moves/succession planning over time.

Transition   Migrate people to different roles to fit their needs/life stage and company needs.

Acquire

Scope Roles

It's critically important to get the role scope right and to get others aligned around that scope. Be clear on the role's responsibilities, authority, and interactions with others. Then get clear on the required strengths, motivation, and fit. Then make sure all the key people that will interact with the new person in this role agree on these. Tool A5.1 can help.

Identify Prospects

Look internally whenever you can. Promoting someone may be the ultimate form of recognition and sends a powerful signal to others in the organization. But, don't compromise. If you have to go outside to get the best people, so be it.

Recruit

Recruit and select using targeted selection or whatever system works for you.

Attract

Candidates can sell themselves first and then do their risk assessment after they've been offered the job. Companies can't flip that switch in reverse. To maximize your chances of attracting candidates when you're recruiting, you must be selling them on how great your organization is even while evaluating them. There is no excuse for not making everyone who interviews with you want to join you, or at least want to refer you to others.

Onboard

Put your new recruits on the road to success even before they start. Make them feel welcome, valued by, and valuable to an organization they can take pride in. High on the list include preparing your own message and touch point plan, encouraging and enabling relationships, and providing your new recruit with help along the way.

Prepare Your Own Message and Touch Point Plan

Start with your own message to new recruits. What do you want them to understand, believe, and do? These might include the context of their role, your vision of success for them, your ideas around their priorities, what capabilities they can access to drive success, and a call to action—what you want them to do first.

Then craft a plan to deliver that message. Manage the welcoming signs and symbols—especially your own time. Model the behaviors and attitudes that you want your new recruits to adopt. Preempt others' potentially counterproductive influence on the new recruit by telling them stories in advance about the organization that help them understand why it is as great as it is.

Follow through with your own media/touch point plan. Think about things like prestart meetings, calls, notes, and packages. Just don't disappear until Day One. If at all humanly possible, be there to welcome new recruits and introduce them on Day One. Investing time in your recruits will help them understand and believe how much you value them.

Encourage and Enable Relationships

As you know, one of the big things new recruits can do between acceptance and their first day on the job is to jump-start key relationships. You can and should help your recruits identify those few most important stakeholders that they should connect with before their first day. Make the introductions. Then get out of the way.

If the position has been open, you've been doing at least part of your new recruit's job. Along the way, you've established relationships with people who are going to be working closely with the new recruit. There is a risk that the strength of your relationships with these people can get in the way of your new recruits' building their own relationships with them. We're not in any way suggesting you hurt these people or damage your relationships with them. Just back off as required so you don't undermine your new recruits' communication or decision flows.

Provide Help

There's no doubt in our completely unbiased minds that giving this book to the people you hire is a great way to help them succeed. The question is when. Giving this book to them the day after they accept the job will allow them to take advantage of the fuzzy front end between acceptance and Day One. Even better would be to give it to them at the time of offering them the job to help them do their own assessment of the risks they're facing. You and your organization will be far better off if your recruits turn down the job, than if they accept a bad match, show up, and fail.

Since we wrote the first edition of *The New Leader's 100-Day Action Plan,* an entire industry has grown up around executive onboarding. Most of the practitioners focus on assimilation coaching—helping new leaders assimilate into their new culture. This is a vital service, but it is not the only assistance that can benefit new leaders. Think in terms of helping your new recruits on three levels: accommodating, assimilating, and accelerating.

Accommodating is all about providing resources to help them get set up in their office and at home—particularly if they are moving. The office part would include desks, computers, phones, PDAs, passwords, and so on. This is relatively straightforward stuff. Just make sure someone is taking care of it.

Assimilating is the next level up. Here you can help them map their stakeholders and make sure they have orientation and onboarding programs and meetings set up, and also have the time to follow through on them.

Accelerating is one more level up. Not every new recruit needs to accelerate their onboarding. Acceleration is not appropriate when the person you hire has a lot of time to learn and the risk of doing something wrong outweighs the risk of not doing something right. In those situations where there is a need for a new person and their team to deliver better results faster, help them follow the program in this book. If it is a particularly hot landing, consider bringing in outside resources to give them extra leverage up front.

Develop

Identify the most important drivers of performance, assess how individuals are doing against them and then develop their skills and knowledge in those areas.

The first complicating factor is time. You've got to strengthen people's skills and knowledge to help them be more successful in their current role *and* prepare them for future roles.

The second piece is assessing their strengths on those key drivers and then choosing which skills and knowledge to invest in. We agree with Gallup's notion that a strength is a combination of talent, skills, and knowledge[1]. Since talent is innate, you can't do anything to build that. So your focus should be on skills and knowledge. The key choice is whether to focus on helping people improve areas that are not strengths or are strengths. Again, we agree with Gallup that helping people get even stronger in areas of strength is more productive than trying to fix their gaps. Far better to find ways to compensate for their gaps.

Encourage

Whoever taught you to say "please" and "thank you" was prescient. This is the key to encouraging people on your team.

"Please" is all about clarity around expectations: objectives, goals, and measures. It's about enabling people to succeed by making sure they have the direction, resources, tools, and support they need and then getting out of their way. (And getting others out of their way.) Big chunks of what we discussed about milestones, in Chapter 11, are applicable here.

"Thank you" is about providing the recognition and rewards that encourage each individual. Herzberg's 1959 work is still applicable.[2] In general, people are positively motivated by things like the type of work they are doing, challenge and achievement, promotion prospects, responsibility, and recognition or esteem. Things like salary, relationship with colleagues, working conditions, and their supervisor's style are "hygiene" factors that don't motivate, but can quickly demotivate if there is a problem.

So the general prescription isn't all that hard. Make sure the hygiene factors are good enough and won't cause problems, and invest in the real motivators. It is not about motivating people. It is about enabling people to succeed so they can tap into their own inner motivations. This enabling point is a big deal. Don't forget it.

You can encourage people to do what you want them to do by clarifying:

- How their individual roles fit with the broader group
- Individual SMART goals (Specific, Measurable, Attainable, Relevant, Time Bound)

---

[1]Marcus Buckingham and Donald Clifton, *Now Discover Your Strengths* (The Free Press, 2001).
[2]Frederick Herzberg, Bernard Mausner, Barbara Block Snyderman, *The Motivation to Work* (New York: John Wiley & Sons, 1959).

- The resources and guidelines required for success
- The link between performance and consequences
- The supporting actions and milestones along the way, in writing
- Required resources

Just as it is important for people to understand how their goals fit with the rest of the organization, it is equally important to make sure people have the resources and support (internally and externally) they need to achieve their goals. It would be silly to ask the sales-force to sell 100 widgets per day with plant capacity of 50 per day. You would end up with unhappy customers, furious salespeople, and nervous breakdowns throughout the plant.

To help reinforce the creation, deployment, and achievement of goals, you need assistance. That assistance comes in the form of seven reinforcements: skills, knowledge, tools, resources, guidelines, the link between performance and consequences, and the actions and milestones along the way.

1. *Skills:* These are the "how-to's" or capabilities. Your goals may be perfect, but you will not reach them without the necessary skills in place. Know what those skills are, and know which ones you have to develop.

2. *Knowledge:* This boils down to facts and experiences that you are aware of. The greater your breadth and depth of knowledge, the higher your chance of reaching your goals.

3. *Tools:* Without the right equipment, you cannot reach your goals. You must know what "equipment is needed," what you have, and how to fill the gap.

4. *Resources:* The three key resource needs are human, financial, and operational. Make sure resources are available to support your established goals in each of these areas. If not, you either have to change your goals to make them more realistic, or increase your access to the needed resource.

5. *Guidelines:* Establish boundaries so everyone knows how far they can run. Know the things that you cannot do.

6. *Link between performance and consequences.* As many organizations get larger and more bureaucratic, they tend to bunch people's annual raises in a narrow range, doing things like giving

those who meet expectations 3–5 percent raises and those who exceed 4–6 percent raises. Over time, this has a devastating effect on performance because people see that they are not going to be rewarded for putting in extra effort to overdeliver and won't get punished for marginal underdelivery.

Make the link between performance and consequences explicit. If that link is properly established, the ratings should be self-evident at the end (e.g., goal: $100MM in sales <80 is below; 80–95 marginally meets; 95–105 meets; 105–120 meets and exceeds; 120+ exceeds).

7. *Actions and milestones along the way.* You cannot do mid-course corrections if you do not know where you're supposed to be at the mid-course. It is far easier to spot a problem when someone says "we produced 9 widgets last month versus a goal of 30," than when someone says "we experienced normal start-up issues but remain fully committed to producing 360 widgets this year." As we saw in Chapter 11, laying out milestones is critical for understanding how to redeploy resources over time to achieve the overall goals.

Plan

Good planning starts with a situational and opportunity assessment. Organizational planning is closely linked with strategic planning. Figure out where you're going and the choices you will implement to get there. Then map out the organization, starting with what it needs to look like in the future state. Armed with that, you can look at people's performance to assess where they are now, where they could get to, and how they can best fit into the future organization.

One CEO told us that some of his people had helped him build the company. They were his most loyal followers. He was their most loyal advocate. But the company outgrew the people and they needed to move to different roles or out.

The organizational evolution curve is very hard to stay ahead of. A little long-term planning can go a long way. Make the mental jump to the organization of the future. Then step back and figure out what you have to do to get there. Some people can grow into their new roles by doing what they're doing now. Some people can grow into their new roles with an investment in their skills and knowledge. Some people can't grow into the roles and will have to be guided in different directions with others slotted in from inside or acquired from outside. This is where tools like Drotter's 9-box matrices are particularly valuable.[3]

And don't forget individual motivation. Some people can get to the place you need them to get to, but they don't want to do so. A good tool for working this through is the "Five-Step Career Plan" from Chapter 1. Have the people that work for you fill this out or update this on an annual basis. It is a useful tool to keep in touch with their own personal long-term goals.

Transition

As discussed in Chapter 13, there are some people moves that you must make quickly. Generally you can evolve people into new roles over time.

Not all transitions are up.

Some people need to move to different roles at the same level to broaden their knowledge or skills or because their existing strengths can make a bigger impact somewhere else.

Some people may want to move down to roles with less scope, responsibility, or stress as they move into different life stages: adding kids, spouse retiring, and so on.

Leadership is about enabling and inspiring others to do their absolute best, together, to realize a meaningful and rewarding shared purpose. If everything stayed constant, people wouldn't have to transition to new roles. Since everything is constantly changing, transitioning people to new roles is often a big part of inspiring and enabling them to do their absolute best.

[3]See Ram Charan, Stephen Drotter, James Noel, *The Leadership Pipeline* (San Francisco: Jossey-Bass, 2001).

Downloadable TOOL A5.1
Role Scope*

Job Title _____

_____

Department_____

_____

Mission/Responsibilities

Why position exists

Objectives/goals/outcomes

Impact on rest of organization

Specific responsibilities

Organizational relationships

Vision

Picture of success

Strengths

Talents (a recurring pattern of thoughts, feeling, or behavior that can be productively applied)

Skills (how-tos, the steps of an activity, capabilities that can be transferred)
—Technical
—Interpersonal
—Business

Knowledge (what you are aware of, facts and lessons learned)
—Required education and training
—Required experience
—Required qualifications

Motivation

How activities fit with person's likes/dislikes/ideal job criteria

How you progress toward long-term goals

Fit

Values

Company/group working style and characteristics

Supervisor working style and characteristics

Approvals

Department manager/supervisor

Buckingham, Marcus, and Donald Clifton. *Now Discover Your Strengths*. New York: Free Press, 2001.

Covey, Steven. *The 7 Habits of Highly Effective People*. New York: Simon & Schuster, 1989.

Duck, Jeannie Daniel. *The Change Monster*. New York: Three Rivers Press, 2001.

Eliot, T. S. "Little Gidding," in *Four Quartets*. New York: Harcourt Brace Jovanovich, 1943.

Gadiesh, Orit, and James L. Gilbert, "A Fresh Look at Strategy." *Harvard Business Review*, May 1998.

Gladwell, Malcolm. *Blink*. Boston: Little, Brown, 2005.

Hilton, Elizabeth. "Differences in Visual and Auditory Short-Term Memory." *Indiana University South Bend Journal*, Volume 4, 2001.

Linver, Sandy. *Speak and Get Results*. New York: Simon & Schuster, 1984.

Lodish, Len. Professor, University of Pennsylvania, Wharton School, conference on October, 1984.

Lombardi, Vince. Legendary Football Coach.

Neff, Thomas, and James Citrin. *You're in Charge, Now What?* New York: Crown, 2005.

Schein, Edgar. *Organizational Culture and Leadership*. San Francisco: Jossey-Bass, 1985.

Senge, Peter. *The Fifth Discipline*. London, UK: Century Business, 1990.

Smart, Brad. *Topgrading*. Englewood Cliffs, NJ: Prentice Hall, 1999.

Watkins, Michael. *The First 90 Days*. Watertown, MA: Harvard Business School Press, 2003.

George B. Bradt has a unique perspective on helping leaders move into complex, high-stakes new roles. After Harvard and Wharton, George spent two decades in sales, marketing, and general management around the world at companies including Unilever, Procter & Gamble, Coca-Cola, and then J.D. Power and Associates as chief executive of its Power Information Network spin-off. Now he is Managing Director of PrimeGenesis, the executive onboarding and transition acceleration group he founded in 2002. George can be reached at gbradt@primegenesis.com.

Jayme A. Check offers a dynamic and global perspective on leadership that he gained from executive roles in both traditional and entrepreneurial environments. His broad-based experience in sales, business development, and general management at companies such as J.P. Morgan, Guidance Solutions, and Brice Manufacturing has given him a unique take on executive acceleration and development. In addition to being a founder of PrimeGenesis and author of its onboarding and transition acceleration methodology, Jayme is also President of Quantum Leap Associates, a firm focused on providing executives worldwide with authentic and measurable leadership skills. Jayme earned a BS from Syracuse University and an MBA from UCLA's Anderson School. Jayme can be reached at JCheck@1QuantumLeap.com or JCheck@primegenesis.com.

Jorge E. Pedraza transitioned from preparing future leaders as a professor at Williams College to being a leader helping build start-ups and reinventing established businesses at Concrete Media, Le Monde Interactive, and Unison Site Management. Jorge has a BA from Cornell and a Yale PhD. As a founding partner of PrimeGenesis, he helped develop and evolve the PrimeGenesis onboarding and transition acceleration methodology and has since deployed it to found and build Unison Site Management, the nation's leading independent cell site acquisition and management company. Jorge can be reached at jpedraza@unisonsite.com.